POSITIVE PARENTING 101

A Handbook for Parents Undergoing Divorce

JAMES A. (JIM) BAKER

FOREWORD BY JOHN BRADSHAW

Bayou
Publishing

HOUSTON, TX

This publication is designed to provide accurate and authoritative information in regard to the subject matter covered. It is sold with the understanding that neither the Publisher nor the Author is engaged in rendering legal, accounting, psychotherapeutic or other professional service. If expert assistance is required, the services of a competent professional person should be sought.

Photos used by permission and licensed by: iStockphoto.com and DepositPhotos.com.

Quantity discounts are available to your company or educational institution for reselling, educational purposes, subscription incentives, gifts or fundraising campaigns. For more information, please contact the publisher at 1-800-340-2034.

Printed in the United States of America   20 19 18 181 7 16 15 14 1 2 3 4 5 6 7 8 9

IISBN: 978-1-886298-35-4   Positive Parenting 101 (pbk)
ISBN: 978-1-886298-67-5   Positive Parenting 101 eBook (ePUB)
ISBN: 978-1-886298-77-4   Positive Parenting 101 eBook (ePDF)

Library of Congress Cataloging-in-Publication Data

Names: Baker, James A., 1943- author.
Title: Positive parenting 101 : a handbook for parents undergoing divorce /
    James A. (Jim) Baker ; foreword by John Bradhsaw.
Description: Houston, TX : Bayou Pub., 2016. | Includes bibliographical
    references and index.
Identifiers: LCCN 2016014038 (print) | LCCN 2016019715 (ebook) | ISBN
    9781886298354 (pbk. : alk. paper) | ISBN 9781886298675 (ePUB) | ISBN
    9781886298774 (ePDF)
Subjects: LCSH: Divorced parents. | Children of divorced parents. |
    Parenting. | Divorce.
Classification: LCC HQ759.915 .B338 2016 (print) | LCC HQ759.915 (ebook) |
    DDC 306.89--dc23
LC record available at https://lccn.loc.gov/2016014038

Bayou Publishing, LLC
2524 Nottingham • Houston, TX 77005-1412
713-526-4558 • http://www.bayoupublishing.com

DEDICATION

I want to express my love and deep appreciation to my smart beautiful wife Xiao Rong Zhang and my delightful, smart, beautiful daughter, Nana, for all of their patience, love and support during this project.

CONTENTS

OVERVIEW

WELCOME TO POSITIVE PARENTING 101!

This 13-lesson handbook has been created to provide parents with the tools needed to effectively parent your children, even in the midst of the turmoil and pain that divorce often brings. For starters, this book will empower you by taking much of the mystery out of parenting. The text explores each major phase in your child's development, and suggests positive ways for you to be a more effective parent in each of those stages.

In addition, this handbook will provide you with important insights for safeguarding and nurturing both yourself and your children during the divorce process. By applying the strategies outlined in this book, you will be laying a strong foundation for growth and healing. Both you and your children will be able to move forward and lead happier, healthier lives.

You may also want to check out the court-approved online course that was designed to accompany this handbook: http://www.online-class-parenting-divorce.com.

FOREWORD

Divorce is a reality in our world, and has been for many generations. As a matter of fact, for many decades now, the divorce rate for all first marriages in the USA has hovered somewhere around 50%. That in itself is a sobering statistic, but one that is all the more troubling when you consider how many children are caught in the middle when families start to fall apart.

Much has been written in recent years about the impact of divorce on children. Some studies seem to indicate that children are likely to suffer long-term negative effects from divorce; others point to hopeful signs that divorce does not have to mean catastrophe for children. That debate will continue to rage for many years. But what should you do right now in your current situation, and how can this book help?

This book is much more practical, facing head-on the reality that divorce does happen, and when it does children are often involved. So, when children are involved, there are steps that parents can and must take to help their children survive the turmoil, regain emotional equilibrium, and adjust to the new world in which they must now live.

Make no mistake about it; this book is first and foremost a book about parenting. There are great strategies and tips in here that will help any parent be a better and more effective parent. But beyond that, this book is intended to help parents continue to nurture, guide and support their children through the chaos that is divorce, which is perhaps the biggest challenge a parent can ever face. I would urge divorcing parents to read this book and follow the guidelines laid out here, if they care about doing what is best for their kids during this traumatic time for everyone.

This simple, helpful handbook is written in a way that is easy to understand and easy to use. I commend my friend, Jim Baker, for once again developing a thorough and very helpful resource that is going to help a lot of people live saner, safer lives.

John Bradshaw
Houston, Texas

INTRODUCTION

Read the following paragraph and see if it strikes a chord in your heart:

> *Children whose parents are going through a divorce almost always feel that they are the cause of the divorce. One of the suggestions in this handbook is that, when telling your children that you and your spouse are divorcing, you should emphasize to them that they are not to blame. In fact, you should let them know in no uncertain terms that they are the best part of your marriage.*

If those words "grab" you, you will appreciate this handbook. You will definitely value its recommendations. The book offers the emotional support and practical help you want and need as a parent who is concerned about the impact divorce is having, or will have, on your children.

If the opening paragraph above does not touch your heart and mind, this handbook will be of even more value to you. The information presented here will alert you to the depths of the challenges you and your children are facing, and help you develop the knowledge and practical "know-how" to help your children get through the emotional upheaval that comes with divorce.

Divorce is a painful time even in the very best of cases. This is especially true when children are involved. All parents, whether they are dealing with divorce or not, want to do a good job of relating to their children and helping them develop emotionally, mentally and physically. Whether you are reading this parenting handbook on your own, or as part of a court-mandated program, you will find that the information contained in this book helps you to effectively parent your children during these difficult times.

The first seven lessons contained in the *Positive Parenting 101* handbook provide a wealth of information, insights, strategies, practices and techniques for building effective parenting skills. The subsequent lessons deal with parenting within the specific context of divorce. These lessons present suggestions and examples on how to take care of your children and yourself during the divorce process, as well as afterward.

Study the recommendations and strategies seriously, and make it your goal to learn and grow. Remember that, in order to make real progress, *you must put what you learn into practice*. Reading the book won't benefit you and your children at all unless you apply what you learn as you interact with your children on a daily basis.

Good luck and Godspeed as you begin your Positive Parenting journey.

Best Regards,
James A. (Jim) Baker

LESSON 1
RESPONSIBLE PARENTING

Divorce is a painful time in the very best of cases. It is emotionally gut wrenching, especially when there are children involved. There are no winners, just survivors.

When people divorce, most experience embarrassment, guilt, and even shame. Among other things, divorcing couples may feel:

- worry that other people may think they didn't try hard enough;

- embarrassment because they are the topic of gossip;

- guilt that they've let their children down;

- a sense of shame at being the cause of the divorce;

- anxiety that their children will be treated differently by other children;

- fear that their children will be forever emotionally damaged by the divorce.

If you are getting a divorce or are already divorced, do not let those feelings keep you from moving forward with your life.

Although some divorced people carry deep emotional scars for the rest of their lives, many find constructive ways to make a good life. Despite having to deal with the hurt, pain, and ego-shattering sense of rejection and loss that can often follow a divorce, they develop meaningful, fulfilling and productive lives.

Which direction will you and your children take? The good news is that it's up to you. It's your decision. You may need some new tactics, though, if the approaches you have been using have not worked very well.

That's what this handbook is about, and that's why you're reading it. Even though divorce is difficult, it doesn't have to be destructive. By studying this book, you will become better able to shepherd yourself and your little ones emotionally through what could otherwise be a devastating experience. You and they can then move forward and lead happier, healthier lives.

Consider two key realities:

1.   Parenting—not the divorce process—is the primary focus of this handbook.

2.   There is life on the other side of the divorce process. You can come out the other end of that stressful, wrenching episode in your life as a stronger person and better parent.

WHAT IS RESPONSIBLE PARENTING?

Parenting is one tough job. The strange thing about parenting is that *the main goal is to make yourself unnecessary*. You want your child to grow into a person who can take care of him or herself. You have about 18 years from start to finish to get the job done.

HANDBOOK GOALS

The goals of this handbook are to:

- present information on how you can become a more effective, positive parent, and demonstrate ways to move your parenting style in that direction;

- examine and explain how parenting techniques need to change as your family copes with divorce;

- provide realistic and practical approaches to good parenting, with simple, understandable explanations and easy-to- remember strategies—with special focus on divorce situations.

PARENTING GOALS

As a parent, you are responsible for providing the necessities of life for each of your children, including meeting emotional, psychological and physical needs.

Your primary goals as a parent are:

- to ensure your child's safety

- to show your child he or she is loved by you

- to teach your child to be self-disciplined

- to teach your child to be self-sufficient

You should view every waking moment as a teaching/learning opportunity. That means you are never "off duty." You must have time to yourself, of course, but what you do with that time is also a teaching opportunity. If you use that time to get drunk or high, you have shown your child that you consider that behavior to be okay.

No doubt about it—selfish, irresponsible or disrespectful behavior will return to haunt you. A child will copy what he sees a parent do. Remember this: *You are the most important example to your child of how a human being is supposed to behave.*

KEEP YOUR CHILD SAFE

Keeping your child safe is not difficult for most parents. Here are some basic safety requirements:

- You must get and use a car seat.

- You must keep unstable or dangerous people out of your home.

- You must not leave your child alone, or with a person you cannot completely trust to care for the child.

- You must not let your child play in the street or other dangerous areas.

You should be following these safety requirements already. If not, you must start immediately.

We assume that you can handle that much. If not, you need to seek help right away. If you cannot provide a safe home for your child, please talk to an officer of the court about the situation.

LOVE YOUR CHILD

It seems like loving your child would be easy. A little baby is so sweet, how can you keep from loving one? But love is not just warm fuzzy feelings. Warm, fuzzy feelings are helpful, but love is much more than that. It is possible to love a person even if you are momentarily annoyed at him or her. When a baby cries most of the night, you still love him or her, even though you may feel exhausted, annoyed, or want to run away and hide. Mixed reactions are understandable.

The same is true when your toddler pulls a lamp off a table, breaking it. You still love him, even though you are upset. Furthermore, when your four-year-old has a whining, crying tantrum in the grocery store while you are trying to shop, buying a candy bar is not the best way to show a four-year-old you love her. It may buy you a few minutes of peace and quiet, but unfortunately it teaches your child that throwing a fit is a good way to get what she wants—that is not love and that is not responsible parenting.

PAY ATTENTION

We will look at specific ways to handle such problems later. Right now, what you need to remember is that, as the parent, what your child needs is not always what he or she wants.

The main things your child needs to know are:

- that you are paying attention;

- that you mean what you say;

- that you will follow through any time you make a promise.

Your child learns these things when you consistently demonstrate them. Paying attention, meaning what you say, and keeping promises will provide the security that is required for a child to feel loved and cared for.

Paying attention may not seem like the most important way to show love. When you think about it, though, how do you *know* that someone loves you? Getting a present does not convince you of a friend's love, if that person really does not want to know what you think or how you feel about things. If he or she prefers not to spend time with you, you can't be sure that person cares about you.

The same is true for a parent. A child who is given all the food, clothes, and toys he could ever want, but never gets the undivided attention of his father, will grow up thinking that Dad does not care about him. That kind of father will spend anything on his child except his own time and attention.

At the other extreme is a father who does not have the money to buy nice clothes and lots of toys for his son, but takes time every day to play ball with him, look at his school papers, tell him about his own childhood, and tuck him in at night. That man's child knows he is loved. It is worth more to him than a closet full of Abercrombies, Nikes, and Transformers.

TEACH YOUR CHILD SELF-DISCIPLINE

How do you teach your child self-discipline? Self-discipline is really self-control. The curious thing is that the more control you can give away, the more you have. The more self-control your child learns, the less you will need to exercise control over your child.

Learning self-control is like learning to walk. First, your tot pushes up to a sitting position, then stands, then holds onto something and takes the first few steps, and eventually toddles across the room alone to fall into your arms. During this learning process, he or she falls many times, gets up to try again, and beams with joy and pride at each little success.

You want your child's efforts at self-control to work the same way. That means you start by helping your child exercise small amounts of self-control to start with, beginning as soon as he can manage them. Let him wipe his high chair tray after he eats—and thank him for doing so. He won't really get it clean, but he will have accomplished something. He learns that what he does makes a difference. That gives a sense of power to the child. Having the power to make a difference is the first step to having control.

Your child cannot learn to exercise control if he or she does not ever get to make choices. Giving children choices of the right kind and as often as possible is a very important tool of good parenting.

TEACH YOUR CHILD SELF-SUFFICIENCY

Self-control and self-discipline are essential to teaching self-sufficiency. Once a child is self-sufficient, you have achieved your primary goal as a parent. Of course, a parent is always needed as a source of encouragement and comfort, so long as the parent lives.

There are many skills needed for self-sufficiency, and parents are the first in a child's life to teach them. Since the most important skill of adulthood is making good choices, wise decision-making is the most important skill to teach your child. Help your child learn to analyze, evaluate, and understand that choices have consequences, some immediate and some long-term.

Congratulations! You have now completed the material for the first lesson. Take the following quiz to check your understanding. If you need to re-read the material above in order to answer any question, please do so.

Lesson 1 Quiz

1.   One of the goals of being a responsible parent is to
      a. *Make sure your child is liked by other kids*
      b. *Ensure your child's safety*
      c. *Do homework for your child, but only once in a while*
      d. *Choose a sport early so he or she can excel in it*

2.   One of the goals of this handbook is to
      a. *Give you suggestions on how to impress the parents of your children's friends*
      b. *Learn how to prevent your child from having a tantrum in the grocery store*
      c. *Examine and explain how your parenting techniques need to change as your family copes with divorce*
      d. *Show you how to stretch your budget for clothes for your child*

3.   Another goal of being a responsible parent is to
      a. *Show you how to "polish" the parenting methods you've been using without much success*
      b. *Prove that infrequent "quality time" with your child is more important than frequent, intentional, heart-to-heart talks with your child*
      c. *Show your child he or she is loved by you*
      d. *Give your child what he or she wants, as long as you can afford it*

4.   Teaching your child self-discipline is
      a. *Strongly related to teaching self-control*
      b. *Well and good if you have time for it, but children can learn it on their own*
      c. *Easier if you model it yourself*
      d. *a and c*

5.   Some people feel embarrassed when they get a divorce because they
      a. *Feel that other people may think they didn't try hard enough*
      b. *Think other people will assume they are always looking for someone to go out with*
      c. *Are the topic of gossip*
      d. *a and c*

6.   T / F   When your child becomes self-sufficient, she won't need you anymore.

7.   T / F   If a child cannot learn self-control in very short order, that's a sign he or she cannot learn it all.

8.   T / F   Learning self-control is like learning to walk; that is, it happens in stages.

9.   T / F   Children are more secure when they know you say what you mean and mean what you say.

10.   T / F   Giving children clothes, treats, and toys is an effective substitute for parental attention.

LESSON 2
FOUR GENERAL STYLES OF PARENTING

Every parent has a unique style of parenting. If yours is not working as well as you would like, it is helpful to look at other ways of parenting. There may be other styles you would like to try. You may not know what will work, but if you know for sure that what is going on now does not work, this is a good time to try something different.

Let's start by looking at various parenting styles and how they affect children.

Parenting styles have been described as falling into four basic groups:

- Drill Sergeant

- Make-Them-Happy

- Uninvolved

- Responsible

These styles each place varying emphases on listening and responding to children, and set different standards for children's behavior. As you consider the various styles of parenting, ask yourself: *Where do I see myself? Which category (or combination of categories) describes how I usually handle my children?*

DRILL SERGEANT PARENTS

The "Drill Sergeant" parent is demanding, results-oriented, and quite strict. The "Drill Sergeant" style is generally too strong in setting standards and too weak in listening and responding. This style of parent usually expects orders to be obeyed without question or explanation. Phrases such as "Because I said so!" and "Just do it!" are common.

The "Drill Sergeant" parent makes a child behave out of fear of punishment, and rarely provides children with choices.

The problem with this style is that the focus is on teaching children to obey authority without question, yet teaching children to *think for themselves* is one of the most important jobs in parenting. Teens who make bad decisions are often making their *first* decisions. They have not had any practice at making decisions. They have not been allowed to make small decisions, where a bad choice does not hurt much. We all need the chance to learn from our mistakes.

Giving a child as many chances as possible to make decisions gives him the opportunity to learn under supervision. Unfortunately, "Drill Sergeant" parents usually do not do a good job of teaching children to think for themselves.

Parents who are controlling and demanding may do responsible things for their kids, but they often don't strive to do things *with* their kids. They also do not teach their children to do things for themselves when they can.

The "Drill Sergeant" parent often uses anger, yelling, and harsh punishment to control the child. Punishing the child by withholding affection is emotional blackmail and only makes the child feel insecure and unloved, with unfortunate and often lasting results.

Children of "Drill Sergeant" parents may appear well behaved, but this is deceptive. The truth is, they usually suffer from lack of self-esteem and often have poor social skills. Not surprisingly, these children often suffer from depression.

They never seem to understand *why* they need to do the things they are told, because they are never given reasons or explanations. Children are curious, and their genuine questions deserve an answer. Very often, they will eventually rebel against the "Drill Sergeant" parent.

Make-Them-Happy Parents

"Make-Them-Happy" parents are weak in setting standards and strong in listening and responding. They may be warm, responsive and very nurturing, but don't enforce rules, standards or conduct. They are inconsistent, highly indulgent and not accountable. They are sometimes called "helicopter parents" because whatever problem their child has, the parents swoop in and fix it for the child.

These parents are responsive, but do not set proper limits. They are also called indulgent, over-protective, or permissive parents, tolerating more negative behavior than is good for the children. With no set boundaries or consistent rules, children often figure out how to control their parents, and are rarely self-reliant.

None of this should be confused with *encouraging independence*. Rather, "make-them-happy" style of parenting means giving up parental responsibility, which these parents consider to be easier than confronting a child's misbehavior and disciplining when necessary.

"Make-Them-Happy" parents often make a rule, but cannot bring themselves to enforce it. In some ways this is worse than not making a rule at all, because it teaches children their parents don't mean what they say. The children keep pushing the parent to set limits, but to avoid confrontation the parent backs down or threatens enforcement "next time."

This practice teaches the child that the parent cannot be depended on, and that the child "deserves to be happy." When the realities of life are inevitably forced on this kind of child, he will find it very difficult to push the boundaries of other authorities the way he has pushed his parents.

A parent who tries to always make the child happy will be pushed to the limit at some point. By then, the parent is so stressed and angry that he or she may transform abruptly into a mean "Drill Sergeant." At that point, the child is really confused, reacting with anger. What transpires is a guaranteed recipe for a classic Spoiled Brat episode.

"Make-Them-Happy" parents interfere and rescue. When a Make-Them-Happy parent's child doesn't follow the rules, skips out on responsibility, or misbehaves, the child knows all he or she needs to do is send up an "I'm in Trouble" flare, and the parents will come flying in to shield him or her from consequences of bad behavior.

The "flying in" image has led some people to call these parents "helicopter" parents, who swoop in to stand between their children and other authorities and protect them from the consequences of their misbehavior.

Children of permissive "Make-Them-Happy" parents remain dependent and don't grow up normally. Children need structure and rules in their lives, even if they rebel against it at times.

Children of "Make-Them-Happy" parents also often tend to perform poorly in school, act more impulsively, and as adolescents they may engage more in misconduct, sometimes including drug use.

UNINVOLVED PARENTS

"Uninvolved" parents are unresponsive, are neglectful and emotionally detached, and make few demands. Many pay little attention to their kids, are not warm, and though they may provide basic needs, they are more concerned with their own needs and desires. Their children do not come first, and suffer because of it.

Children from "uninvolved parents" feel unimportant and unwanted. Because they don't feel loved, they have problems loving and feeling good about themselves. Consequently, they usually have problems developing necessary social skills. A few do their best to provide for themselves, and some may end up wiser and more independent than their years. However, these few are the exceptions.

With "Uninvolved" parents, the parenting goals of developing self-discipline and self-sufficiency do not get met, so their children continue to be needy and frustrated. The skills a person needs for coping with the difficulties of life are not taught to or developed in the child. Unfortunately, as the child grows up, refuge is often sought in alcohol or drugs to escape the pain of being unable to cope.

Alcohol, drug abuse and other addictive behaviors are rampant among "Uninvolved" parents. These people have serious problems of their own, and are ill equipped to deal with the demands of raising children.

Children of "Uninvolved" parents learn early that Mom and Dad really aren't interested in what they have to say, or in how they feel. It doesn't take long to get the message. As a consequence, these children pull back and don't even think of confiding in their parents.

RESPONSIBLE PARENTS

"Responsible" parents set and enforce high standards for their children, and are also warm, responsive, and attentive to them. As a result, they tend to produce self-reliant children—and children who are healthy and happy. Obviously, the goal in rearing your children is to be a "Responsible" parent.

To be a "Responsible" parent, keep in mind these four main goals:

1. Ensure your child's safety,

2. Show your child he or she is loved by you,

3. Teach your child to be self-disciplined,

4. Teach your child to be self-sufficient.

"Responsible" parents give their child chores to do, but exercise good judgment and common sense in doing so. The parent does not ask Junior or Suzy to wash the good china at the age of three. They will help Junior learn to do things for himself, but will not let him climb up on the roof to retrieve a toy airplane at the age of four. They will consider his or her safety at all times.

They also teach small steps in becoming self-sufficient. They make sure the outcome of any failure by the child is not too serious until the child learns to make good choices. A child who has never made small decisions for herself will often go drastically wrong when she finally gets a chance to make major choices.

Choosing friends at the age of 13 has much more potential for danger than choosing clothes at age four. Start small, keep increasing the responsibility, and watch your child learn to make good choices. Talk about the choices, letting the child tell you why she is choosing one thing over another. ***Never give a child a choice you cannot let her make.***

A "Responsible" parent shows the child he or she is loved, and demonstrates that by giving a child frequent eye contact, soft words, tender hugs, and words of encouragement. The parent praises the child when he or she does something well, and calmly corrects his or her mistakes.

The parent also makes a conscious effort to help the children learn independence. Like learning to walk, children learn independence a little bit at a time. The child will make mistakes and learn from them.

If a toddler is headed for a blazing fireplace, the parent scoops up the child, points out the danger, and makes sure he/she doesn't get near it again. If Suzy heads toward a busy street, they stop her. However, they do not prevent her from running around in the park just because she might trip and fall. They let a child take *reasonable risks* in order to learn.

Responsible parents will also establish *consequences*. Make sure the child understands the consequences of bad behavior before it occurs. Every child misbehaves on occasion. It's important that parents respond consistently in requiring the child to suffer the consequences of his or her poor choices.

A child reaching school age needs to learn to get up in the morning and get ready for school. If Suzy does not get up when her alarm goes off, dawdles over her breakfast, or won't put on her clothes, she must learn a lesson. She must be told what time she must be ready, and if she is not, her parents must be willing to make her face the consequences.

A responsible parent teaches time management to the child by helping him or her practice it, not by forcing it. That way the child has accomplished something, and feels more independent, and thus more "grown up." Every child wants to be "grown up," and every child must learn that the real meaning of being "grown up" is to be self-controlled and self-sufficient.

Responsible Parents help the child take reasonable risks in order to learn. In every parenting situation, you want to do three things:

1. Pay attention

2. Mean what you say

3. Follow through

Generally, "Responsible" parents tend to produce capable and successful children. That's because they balance *clear demands* with *emotional responsiveness*, while still recognizing the need for children to know they are loved even when they are being punished. This results in well-adjusted, well-behaved, resourceful children. It shouldn't come as any surprise that research indicates these children are the highest achievers of any group.

The four general types of parents are broad categories. You may fit in one category on one day and a different category on another day. Be honest with yourself. Where do you fit? What group or groups do you fall into? How badly do you want to change?

The following quiz will help you to review Lesson 2, which covered parenting styles.

LESSON 2 QUIZ

1.   DRILL SERGEANT parents
     a. Are too strong in setting standards and too weak in listening and responding
     b. Are too strong in setting standards and go overboard in listening and responding
     c. Are too weak in setting standards and go overboard in listening and responding
     d. Are too weak in setting standards and too weak in listening and responding

2.   MAKE-THEM-HAPPY parents
     a. Are too strong in setting standards and too weak in listening and responding
     b. Are too strong in setting standards and go overboard in listening and responding
     c. Are too weak in setting standards and go overboard in listening and responding
     d. Are too weak in setting standards and too weak in listening and responding

3.   UNINVOLVED parents
     a. Are too strong in setting standards and too weak in listening and responding
     b. Are too strong in setting standards and go overboard in listening and responding
     c. Are too weak in setting standards and go overboard in listening and responding
     d. Are too weak in setting standards and too weak in listening and responding

4.   RESPONSIBLE parents
     a. Are strong in setting standards and strong in listening and responding
     b. Are too strong in setting standards and go overboard in listening and responding
     c. Are too weak in setting standards and go overboard in listening and responding
     d. Are too weak in setting standards and too weak in listening and responding.

5.   Children who are resourceful and have high self-esteem are probably the product of which parenting style?
     a. Drill Sergeant
     b. Make-Them-Happy
     c. Uninvolved
     d. Responsive

6.   Impulsive children who don't learn self-control are typically a product of which parenting style?
     a. Drill Sergeant
     b. Make-Them-Happy
     c. Uninvolved
     d. Responsible

7.   Parents who are warm and nurturing but don't enforce rules are usually:
     a. Drill Sergeant
     b. Make-Them-Happy
     c. Uninvolved
     d. Responsible

8.   Parents who explain things to children, are highly responsive, and are nurturing even when a child misbehaves are:
   a.   *Drill Sergeant*
   b.   *Make-Them-Happy*
   c.   *Uninvolved*
   d.   *Responsible*

9.   In any parenting situation, which should you not do?
   a.   *Pay attention*
   b.   *Mean what you say*
   c.   *Follow through*
   d.   *Send the child to the other parent*

10.   T / F   Children are more secure when you say what you mean and you mean what you say.

LESSON 3
BECOMING THE PARENT YOU WANT TO BE

Parents don't usually set out to follow the "Drill Sergeant," "Make-Them-Happy," or "Uninvolved" parenting styles. No one wants his or her child to grow up with poor self-esteem, bad behavior, or poor social skills. So how do these things happen?

Simply put, we do what we know. Some of us simply don't have the correct tools in our parenting toolbox. Perhaps you don't want to do what your own parents did, but many times, you end up repeating their very actions. This usually happens until you are provided with new approaches, which work better.

Remember, the goal is to help you learn to use a positive, responsible parenting style. Perhaps you are already a "Responsible" parent to some degree. If you are already focused on the four goals of providing safety, love, self-discipline, and self-sufficiency, this handbook will help you polish your skills. If you have not been focused on those goals, this is your chance to learn this positive approach.

ADVICE FROM THE PROS

Television's Judge Hatchett says that "if you're really committed to changing your life, to walking a better road, all it takes is a change in direction and a commitment to that change in direction. Turn the corner, and keep walking, and after a while you look back over your shoulder and you can no longer see the old road. After a while, that new path—New Hope Road—becomes the only way."

Another parenting expert and author explains that "parenting groups are great places to learn new skills and ideas and to get moral support along the way. But when all is said and done, parenting is essentially a matter of the heart and spirit as well as training and knowledge—it's all too easy to lose sight of our love for our children when they continually misbehave in ever-more-inventive ways."

FIRST STEPS TO POSITIVE PARENTING

So let's look at how you can begin to make some changes. It can be done right now as you read this handbook. You really *can* do it; and it's not as difficult as you might think.

When parents learn and apply new child-rearing strategies and techniques, they soon find their so-called "problem children" become more cooperative, happier children. When parents learn what motivates children and realize they can use parenting tools they didn't have before, they gain confidence. When parents are more confident and secure in what to do and how to do it, positive things happen.

After you have *changed* your parenting style, the next steps are *follow-through* and consistency, which are especially important when a family is in the midst of a divorce.

If you are willing to change to a new style of parenting, but feel it may be hopeless, do not despair. Do not expect an overnight transformation either; just remain confident that changes will happen.

BEGIN WITH SMALL STEPS

Start with just one behavior that needs adjustment. The bedtime routine might be a good place to start. First, decide clearly what changes need to be made. Then make a list on paper, or at least in your head. This list might include:

- Gather all school supplies, books, and papers, and put each child's stack in a designated place.

- See that each child has laid out the clothes that he or she will put on the next morning.

- Tell your child exactly what the new routine will be. You may want to make a song or chant out of it, as you will repeat it every night for years, sometimes more than once. It might be something like, "PJs, teeth, potty, water." The children should complete this routine before story time or before any other "treat" occurs.

- Do not insist that the children must "Go to sleep *now*." You cannot force him or her to sleep. Don't try to fight that battle, as long as the child is in bed with the lights out. Do insist on Junior getting up the next morning at the right time. If he is sleepy because he chose to play with toy soldiers under the covers late into the night, just say, "Yeah, I know how hard it is to get going when I don't get enough sleep." Leave it at that, and let him figure out what to do about it. Having a choice in the matter can help him accept responsibility for his actions.

- Do not refuse your child a night-light, a favorite blanket, or stuffed animal. Do not dismiss such things as "childish." Things that reinforce a child's security are very important to him.

CHANGING YOUR APPROACH

When progress has been made on one front, begin to tackle another. Remember that your children won't change unless your approach changes first. Try changing the tone of voice you use with your children. Remember you should *never yell at them or demean them*. Then you can work on specific situations with your children.

Follow-through is especially important when you change parenting styles, and expect your children to maintain good behavior and habits, especially when you are in the midst of a divorce. Responsible parenting is a long-term process.

When a divorce occurs, parenting becomes more difficult. Children react to emotional pain in different ways. Some internalize the hurt and withdraw into themselves. Some act out. Others appear to be fine, but inside they are struggling to hold themselves together because they feel responsible for the break-up.

Some people believe that children can never cope healthily with divorce, that it becomes a psychological life sentence. However, it doesn't have to be! Psychologist Randy Cale explains that when parents handle things properly, divorce can be like breaking a bone. When well cared for, the break hurts for a period of time, but as it heals, it can become even stronger than the original bone.

It's all up to you: If you work at it, you can lessen the impact of the divorce on yourself, your children, and your spouse. If you really try, you can rise to the challenge and help your children survive and thrive in what can otherwise be a confusing and traumatic, even devastating experience.

In any environment, the physical, mental and emotional well-being of children is directly linked to the sense of security and self-esteem they receive from their parents. *The most important security builders for children are being held, loved, smiled at, talked to, played with, and listened to.* As children grow, they also need positive physical affection, encouraging words, and age-appropriate discipline in order to establish the sense of security and self-worth needed for them to remain emotionally healthy.

Responsible parents permit children to ask questions, but in the end, the parents are the final decision-makers in the household. Those parents expect positive results from their children, but reach this objective by guiding their children through *discussion* and *involvement*. Usually their children are very social, do well in school, and have high self-esteem. They are more likely to be competent, have high leadership qualities, and do well with original thinking and concepts.

Naturally, these are all fine qualities that all of us want for our children to have. The question is, "How do we get there from here?"

Do you feel like you are always saying "no" and shouting at your children—who don't listen anyway? Are you constantly making threats that your kids ignore? These approaches are total failures, aren't they? They're not getting you anywhere, nor are they helping your kids.

You need to adopt new strategies to meet the goals of responsible parenting. Remember, the goals of responsible parenting are to:

- Ensure your children's *safety*

- Show your children they are *loved* by you

- Teach your children to be *self-disciplined*

- Teach your children to be *self-sufficient*.

HAVE HIGH EXPECTATIONS

Responsible parents have high expectations for their children. The parent who expects that Junior will be a "worthless good-for-nothing just like his dad" will get just what she expects. The parent who expects Suzy to grow up to be a fine young woman who can achieve anything will get a better result.

Just hoping for greatness won't make it happen. If you encourage the child to dream big and aim high, though, the odds are much better for high achievement.

Judge Hatchett, of the popular TV series, identifies some strategies for parents who aim to raise smart, safe, successful children. According to her, the best strategies are to:

- Expect greatness

- Keep your word

- Listen carefully

If you practice doing those three things, your children will learn that you love them and will trust you to help them learn to be independent.

You must have high expectations for yourself, as well. You must supervise this crucial project of growing a new adult with consistency, kindness, and courage. Sure, you will make mistakes. When you do, admit it, ask forgiveness, and keep on trying. A little humor is also a big help. The more you talk about the challenges and rewards of responsible parenting with your friends, the more support you will find.

GIVE LOTS OF ENCOURAGEMENT

It is important to offer encouragement to your children at every opportunity*.* As they grow secure in the knowledge that you love them and that you are trying to teach them the things they need to succeed, they also need to be encouraged to keep trying.

Paying attention to your children is absolutely essential. Any child who says "Mama" more than three times in a row is potentially in trouble. *You need to acknowledge that child.* It may mean reaching over and putting a gentle hand on the child and saying, "Wait, please," but the child should know he or she is not ignored.

The parent must emphasize and reinforce, as early as possible, that only in an emergency should the child interrupt when Mom is talking to another person who is present or on the phone.

A good practice for Junior to get Mom or Dad's attention is for Junior to gently put his hand on Mom or Dad's hip and stand there until the parent can acknowledge him. The child should not noisily clamor for attention. Even if the child is patient and polite, the parent still needs to turn their attention to the child at the first opportunity. If a child has to yell or throw a fit to get a parent's attention, that parent is not doing a good job.

Life, as we all know, is not easy. Living through a divorce is especially difficult. When you are feeling sad and down, and maybe even fearful of the future, it is hard to be constantly on the parenting job. Sometimes it may be hard to be an encouraging parent. But always do your best to offer a "Good job" or just a high five as often as you can. And try to have a smile for your children, even though you might be feeling sad at the moment.

You will not perform perfectly 100% of the time. Give yourself credit for making the effort. Remember that every success you establish puts your whole family a step closer to good emotional health. Know that the most responsible parents on the planet do not do everything right every time. You are not a bad parent if you make mistakes here and there. You are facing many difficulties. Trying to improve your parenting practices while suffering an emotional shipwreck is asking a lot of yourself. But it's important to constantly analyze what you're doing, how you're doing it, and what you want for your children.

Many parents don't realize how much of an impact they have on their children. They understand how their actions affect their children "in the now," but often overlook the effect they have on their children's future.

Sometimes your parenting efforts won't work out as you planned. When that happens, it's okay to say, "Well, that didn't work as well as I had hoped."

That isn't a bad thing to say to the child, either. As you talk about problem behavior, there are times when a heart-to-heart about behaviors, consequences, and rewards can be very helpful. If your teen wants a later curfew, it is worth a serious discussion. Find a time to really talk it through together. You can reach agreement on items such as:

- You don't want to be awake half the night worrying about her safety

- She doesn't want to look like a baby to her friends

- You don't want her to be out on the road late at night

- She wants to be free to "be herself"

The degree to which she has demonstrated responsibility and maturity will guide what you feel safe to allow. Mistakes and bad decisions on her part will shrink the amount of freedom she gets to keep. Good decisions will increase her freedom. Remember, the goal is to help her learn to make good decisions and be a responsible adult later. Work for positive outcomes: Nothing is more encouraging than success.

Every child needs love and affection. The younger the child is, the less likely he or she is to think he doesn't need it. Take every opportunity to offer your child eye contact, a gentle touch, a hug, a high five, or whatever he or she accepts as a sign of affection. A wink at the right time, or a thumbs up as they leave for school, can help a day start better. A note in a lunch sack for older kids is a good idea, especially on a day that you know is going to present extra challenges.

CONSEQUENCES

A consequence is a natural result of an action. When you put a pan of water on the fire, it gets hot. If you stick your hand in very hot water, it will burn you. This is not a *punishment*; it is a *consequence* of putting your hand in the wrong place. When a parent uses consequences to teach self-control, the consequence should be a logical and natural result of the behavior. *It should not be a punishment that is unrelated to the behavior.*

Remember to consider the desired goal of assigning the consequence. Are you just trying to show Junior who's boss, or do you want him to learn to get his homework done before bedtime? Showing a child you have power over him is not a good goal. You want him to learn to take the power over himself and to do the right thing.

A parent may need to help his or her child learn to get off to school efficiently by making a checklist of things to be done the night before. If he or she fails to follow through on the routine and goes to school without her lunch, the natural *consequence* is that your child will have to be hungry that day. However, if a child throws a toy at a playmate, going without her supper would not be a natural consequence, but a *punishment*. Make sure that consequences are logical and related to the action. Natural consequences in this case might include removing the toy and ending the play session.

GIVE YOUR CHILD STRUCTURE

The more structure your child has in his or her life, the more effective this kind of discipline will be. Junior and Suzy already know that there are rewards and consequences. If Suzy has experienced reasonable rewards and consequences from her actions all along, she will expect more of the same. If her life has been unpredictable all along, she will not know what to expect or how to learn from what happens.

You want your child to know that effort produces better results than laziness, that kindness will get better results than rudeness, and that if you break the rules, there will be a price to pay.

At the same time, you should demonstrate to your children the concept of grace. Perhaps Suzy wants you to bail her out of her own mistakes frequently, while you know she needs to live with the consequences or she won't learn to make better choices. You might consider an agreed-upon "Get Out of Jail Free Card" system. Perhaps she can use the parental safety net once during each six weeks, but that's it. One is all she gets.

Stand firm. If she's already used up her grace card for the six weeks and then forgets her permission slip, she may have to stay in study hall while the class goes on the field trip. She may have to skip eating lunch if she forgets her lunchbox. She will learn to think ahead, or make notes for herself, or tie a red ribbon on her backpack to remind herself to check her list each morning. You can help her brainstorm ways to remind herself. You can plan a special reward if she accumulates grace cards that she does not use.

Rewards are an important part of teaching with consequences. If Junior's math grades are slipping because he is not finishing his homework, he may lose privileges to such distractions as the TV, computer, or Game Boy for two weeks. But once the teacher reports that he is completing his work and his grades have improved, he gets his game time back, and a trip to the ice cream stand, or his favorite dessert for supper, or a paint ball session.

Do not buy your teenager a new car because he made an A in P.E. Rewards must fit your budget and be appropriate for the child, and as a part of the consequences system, they must be logical. *Never use a reward as a bribe.*

MAKE A LIST

A useful exercise for parents is to sit down and make a list of consequences and rewards that would be appropriate for each child in the family. You need mild ones, severe ones, and in-between ones. They might range from starting homework 30 minutes after arriving home instead of after supper, to losing TV or cell phone privileges for several days. Rewards might include a half hour of shooting baskets with Dad, or making cookies one Saturday with Mom, or a sleepover at Grandma's.

You must apply the consequence to every infraction of the set rule. It is the same as keeping any other promise. Your child must know, without a doubt, that you will enforce the promised consequences for the infraction. That is how discipline teaches self-control and reinforces security in the child. On the rare occasions that you may offer an occasional exemption, it must be agreed on ahead of time. Otherwise you are not keeping your part of the bargain.

What skills do your children need in order to be fully functioning individuals? Children need to learn to take care of themselves. It is your job to teach them, over time, to help keep the house presentable, clean floors and bathrooms, cook for themselves, clean the kitchen after meals, do their own laundry, keep the yard, understand basic car care, sew on buttons, keep a checkbook, and other basic skills that grownups know how to do.

Children should not try to gain all those skills the summer before they move out on their own or go off to college. They need to acquire these skills gradually as they grow up, helping Mom or Dad in the house, yard, and garage. These are times of sharing and learning. Acquiring such skills should not be forced on the child, but offered as opportunities to do something with a parent.

Another skill is one you must practice and always adhere to: **You must never handle your child in anger.** If you cannot control yourself, send the child to his room and go to your own, with the agreement to meet in the kitchen when a timer goes off. You cannot teach a child to practice self-control if you cannot demonstrate that you have it yourself.

BE CONSISTENT AND FAIR

You must practice consistency, fairness, and kindness. When Junior has been ugly to Suzy, you do not yell, "Don't yell at your sister!" You should calmly tell him you are disappointed in how he is treating his sister, that it will not be allowed, that he must apologize. Calmly tell him he must then miss the next TV show he was going to watch, or give up his turn on the computer to her, or make amends in some way that costs him something and gives something to her. This assumes, of course, that she has not retaliated in kind. In that case, they should apologize to each other and both miss out on TV or game time or dessert. The old-fashioned consequence of sitting in the corner or taking a "time out" can be appropriate at some ages. Customarily, one minute per year of age is appropriate for such "power breaks," such that a 7 year-old child might take a cool-down break for 7 minutes.

Having the list of possible consequences comes in handy for discipline on the fly. You don't have to stop and rack your brain for an appropriate consequence. In fact, your kids can probably help you make the list, if you do it at a time when no one is in trouble.

TEACH YOUR CHILD TO SOLVE PROBLEMS

Life is full of problems. The optimistic person sees them as challenges, or learning opportunities, and finding the solutions as interesting instead of scary. Helping your child learn to approach life that way is one of the greatest gifts you can give him.

To solve a problem or challenge, you first need to recognize it for what it is. For a child who has trouble getting ready for school in time, you will want to sit down together when you are both in a good mood and ask questions such as, "What do you need to do each morning to get ready for school? What time do you think you need to get up to get all that done without having to rush?" You might help the child make a list of tasks, with estimates of time for each.

Being self-disciplined means taking responsibility for those things that you should be doing. Thinking through the steps of solving a problem gives your child a feeling of confidence. With a solution in hand, the "problem" becomes more of a challenge instead.

Self-discipline is essential to success in any endeavor. Even lots of talent will not bring success if that talent is not managed well, and it takes self-discipline to do that.

When the child has mapped out a plan, give high fives and encouragement. Ask him or her how the plan is working after it gets implemented. It may need some revisions, such as allowing more time for some items.

Congratulations! You have now finished Lesson 3. The following quiz will check what you've learned about becoming the parent you want to be.

LESSON 3 QUIZ

1.   The most effective parenting style is
   a. *Uninvolved*
   b. *Responsible*
   c. *Make-Them-Happy*
   d. *Drill Sergeant*

2.   Some key elements of becoming a responsible parent are
   a. *Encouragement*
   b. *High Expectations*
   c. *Using Consequences to teach self-control*
   d. *All of the above*

3.   When it comes to parenting, "Responsible" parents
   a. *Always get it right*
   b. *Spend a great deal of time and effort trying to get it right*
   c. *Ask their neighbors what is right*
   d. *All of the above*

4.   Judge Hatchet says that to be a good parent you should
   a. *expect greatness*
   b. *keep your word*
   c. *listen carefully*
   d. *all of the above*

5.   Some of the skills parents should help their children acquire while they are growing up are
   a. *cleaning the house*
   b. *cooking for themselves*
   c. *keeping their own checkbook*
   d. *all of the above*

6.   T / F   Bribes are okay, if they keep your child happy.

7.   T / F   Your teen's request for a later curfew is worth talking about seriously.

8.   T / F   How a child turns out has nothing to do with how you expect them to turn out.

9.   T / F   There are times when a heart-to-heart talk about acceptable ways to behave, consequences, and rewards can be very helpful.

10. T / F   Rewards are an important part of teaching consequences.

LESSON 4
PARENTING PRE-SCHOOL CHILDREN

AFFECTION

Love your babies all the time. Cuddle them as much as you can. Carry them with you where you can touch and talk to them. If you must leave a little one with another caregiver, choose carefully. Do not leave your child with a care-giver who is curt or mean. Find someone who is warm, friendly, and responsible. You want to have your standards of behavior reinforced, but your child needs to feel *cared about* as well as *cared for*. If you see any evidence that your child is not being treated well, find another person immediately.

BASIC COMMANDS

When you have your youngster with you, be prepared to teach basic good behavior. By the age of eighteen months, a child should be able to obey some basic instructions.

In *Parenting with Love and Logic*, the authors say that most normal children of this age understand simple words like "come" and "sit" and know exactly what we want when we say them. They call this "Basic German Shepherd."

When a toddler disobeys a basic instruction, he or she should be moved away to stand or sit in a corner in the same room with the parent. The parent briefly and calmly explains that the child must obey when told to "Stop" or "Go" or "Sit." A couple of minutes is sufficient for this.

If a child persistently disobeys and is disruptive, remove the child to another room. Do not send a very young child to be alone. You want the child to feel a *separation* from the current activity, but not *abandonment* by the parent. If several rehearsals of this do not bring obedience, increase the amount of time out, but do not show anger. Teach calmly and give affection afterward. You want the child to learn to mind you so that he can learn to do bigger things safely. When he does obey, be lavish with praise. *A child will learn more quickly from praise of successful obedience than from punishment of failure.*

There are different schools of thought on the efficacy and advisability of spanking. Many parents do not believe in corporal punishment of any kind. For parents who do choose to spank, it is critical that the punishment must not be severe, and must not be delivered in anger. If you have the necessary self-control to deliver mild physical punishment without overdoing it, you may find that after one or two episodes of spanking, you will not have to resort to it again. Often, the mere suggestion of spanking as a possible consequence for refusal to obey will get the child to respond.

BEDTIME

At bedtime, sharing a "happy time" of the day is a good idea. You will want to share something of your day with them. You may remind the child of a time during the day when he or she made you proud by being obedient. This is a good time to reinforce positives. You may be surprised by some of the things you learn in those talks.

Bedtime is an especially important time of the day for toddlers. The routine of getting ready for bed should be well ingrained by the time a child is ready for kindergarten. Having conquered P.J.'s "teeth, potty, water, and story" will give a child confidence she can master the list for getting off to school.

If you have been taking your child to day-care, you should have a routine for that as well. As she gets older, more of her "to-do" list should become her responsibility. For her, starting kindergarten or first grade will be no big deal. But you owe it to her to be teaching the routine from the first day she spends away from the house.

CHORES

Even small children should have chores to do at home. Many parents want to skip this, because it is easier to just do it rather than to have a child "mess it up." But a child needs to contribute to the family and needs to learn to do things for himself.

An eight-year-old child who has never swept the kitchen or unloaded the dishwasher is a neglected child. Children should have started learning to help at a much younger age.

A toddler cannot unload the dishwasher, but he can help take his plastic plate to the counter after eating, or bring the forks and spoons from the table to the sink. If a child can walk, he or she can pick up toys and put them back where they belong.

Part of your job is to organize the child's toys in a manner that he can recreate when putting them away. If all you need is for them to be off the floor, get a laundry basket for him to pile them in. Low shelves will also work just fine.

Make dessert wait until the chore is done, or offer some other treat as a reward. Every time you are obeyed is a step up. Always remember to say, "Good job!"

Help your child to perform a chore a few times, and then expect him or her to do it alone. Don't think that you shouldn't have to praise your child for what he "ought" to do anyway. You are *teaching*, and praise is an incentive to do the right thing. Eventually, he will do it without needing praise. By then he'll be working on something much more difficult, but he'll be working on it with confidence, because he's already succeeded at some smaller things.

If an accident happens and your child knocks his milk over, don't scold. Help him learn to clean it up. Show the child that accidents are normal, mistakes are okay, and that you are here to help him learn from these things. It is not your job to shame or blame when a child spills his milk. It's your job to show your child what to do the next time it happens, or how to take steps to prevent it. If such spills happen more than twice, get him a cup with a lid. Until he can avoid accidents, it would be better to help your child avoid the embarrassment, the mess, and the waste.

WHINING

The fastest way to deal with whining is not to hear it. Really! When your child starts to whine, tell him or her, "I can't hear you when you whine. Can you think of another way to say that?" You will be amazed how quickly whining stops when you use this script and simply don't respond to the content of the whine.

MELTDOWNS AND MISBEHAVIOR

And what about "meltdowns?" Children experience the same feelings that adults do, but have limited language and communication skills. They need to be taught to control their behavior in response to those feelings. *"Meltdowns"* are a result of feelings they cannot control, such as frustration and disappointment. The grocery store is a classic place for a meltdown, but there is a technique for dealing with it. The technique has three parts:

1. Prevent the problem if you can

2. Stop and pay attention

3. Help the child find a solution

Preventing the grocery store meltdown might be as easy as leaving the child with a neighbor while you shop. If that is not possible, think ahead before stopping at the store. If the child is tired and hungry at that time of day, you are asking for trouble just by going to the store.

Head problems off by giving the child a snack when you put him or her in the shopping cart. Tell your child that when you get to the store you will give him a bag of crackers to snack on while you shop. Plan to have a plastic zipper bag which contains crackers or raisins or other finger foods that are not going to be a choking hazard or create messy fingers—or look like you picked them out at the store.

After a couple of trips to the store, your child will expect to snack while you shop. The snack will keep your child busy, and make him feel less hungry and tired. That is a positive way to arrange a less stressful stop at the grocery store. It should be presented to the child with instructions to help you get the shopping done quickly.

If the snack is eaten and your child starts whining anyway, your first job is to listen to the child. If he or she is asking for a toy from the store shelf, push right on past it while you talk about which toy at home he or she will want to play with when you get there. Sometimes, having the parent's attention and being talked *with*—rather than *to*—is enough to distract the child from having a tantrum.

The point of such a distraction is to help the child learn self-discipline. He or she will learn to control him- or herself as you help your child figure out ways to do it. Taking your mind off what is bothering you by focusing on something else works for you, doesn't it? It will also work for your child, in most cases.

If you cannot prevent the tantrum and your attention does not keep it from erupting, you must deal with it. You should remove the child from the cart. Lead her outside and stand with her on the sidewalk. Get down on your child's level and look her in the face. Stay calm. The child is already out of control. It certainly doesn't help her if the parent loses control as well.

Tell your child that throwing a fit is not going to be allowed from now on. Talk as softly as you can. She will have to get quiet to hear what you are saying. It is not a good idea to give her what she is demanding. The fact that she is demanding it is enough reason to deny the request. Do not let her manipulate you into buying a toy or a treat.

You might make an offer to get the desired treat if she earns it by finishing this trip calmly and behaving well the next time. Remind her of this promise the next time you need to stop at the store. If she is very young and you can manage to make the next stop a short one, you will have a good chance of avoiding future grocery store meltdowns.

Now you have completed Lesson 4. Here is the quiz over this lesson.

LESSON 4 QUIZ

1. Which goal is not part of responsible parenting?
    a. *To ensure your child's safety*
    b. *To show your child he or she is loved by you*
    c. *To make sure your child believes you are a better parent than your ex-spouse*
    d. *To teach your child to be self-disciplined*

2. An appropriate response to a meltdown is to
    a. *Try to prevent the problem by anticipating stressful triggers*
    b. *Distract the child if you notice your child is winding up*
    c. *Talk with your child about other ways to solve the problem*
    d. *All of the above*

3. What is a useful bedtime routine?
    a. *Sharing a "positive/happy time" and a "negative/sad time"*
    b. *Listing all your child's faults so they can be corrected*
    c. *None, because routines are bad*
    d. *None of the above*

4. T / F   TV's Judge Hatchett believes divorcing parents have an opportunity to change their lives, which is the chance to choose a path she calls "New Hope Road."

5. T / F   It is important to offer encouragement to your children at every opportunity.

6. T / F   A consequence is a natural result of an action.

7. T / F   Parents are not responsible for teaching children self-sufficiency skills.

8. T / F   Affection is a basic need of pre-school children.

9. T / F   Even small children should have chores to do at home.

10. T / F   Whining and meltdowns are normal responses to stress, but it is possible for your child to learn other, more productive responses.

LESSON 5
PARENTING ELEMENTARY SCHOOL CHILDREN

Responsible parenting strategies do not change when children start school. They just get more complex. The basics remain the same. Your goals are still to keep the child safe, show him or her your love and concern, and teach self-discipline leading to self-sufficiency.

Routines are more important than ever. They provide stability and predictability. In our world of uncertainty, and especially during a divorce, routine is important to both children and adults. It reassures us that the world is safe and drives away the chaos that often accompanies major changes.

CHOICES

You should empathize with the consequences that come from a bad choice. If Suzy brings home a very bad spelling test, you can say sympathetically, "I'll bet it was embarrassing to have your teacher see that you did not study enough for that test." Give her time to think about or respond to this, and then ask, "What are you going to do about it?"

You can and should spend time asking questions that require your child to think about his choices. Encourage him to consider what to do about problems that are the consequence of making the wrong choice. Then stop talking about it. Do not always provide the answer, or insist that the child give you the answer you're hoping for right away.

Remember never to propose a choice that you cannot allow the child to make. You can offer Suzy the choice of going with you to visit an elderly neighbor, or staying with a friend down the street (whose parent you know is home) while you make the visit. You do not offer to let Suzy hang out at the convenience store because she is uncomfortable with old Mrs. Jones and all her medical equipment.

Choices of entertainment become much bigger issues in elementary school. The parents of many of your child's friends may have different standards for what their kids watch on television, or which movies they view. You need to have very firm ideas of what you believe is appropriate. You are probably already aware that the moral tone of broadcast TV is lower than ever, even in so-called "family hours."

You cannot protect your children from harsh realities and ugly situations forever, but do not allow them to be exposed to detrimental media until it just can't be helped. Any time and every time you have a choice about what your children will see and hear, enforce your standards simply because they are your standards, and you are the parent.

Your child may object like crazy when you tell her she can't watch something that her friends watch, but when she is older, she may confess that now she understands and thinks you did the right thing.

Your pre-teen needs to take responsibility for more chores, and should get more significant rewards. Your children should help with yard care and in the kitchen. In fact, there will come a time when your children can prepare a meal without much supervision from you. They should have been trained in the safe use of kitchen tools and appliances.

A well-trained eight-year-old can get up early to cook muffins for Mom's birthday. A six-year-old can make his own peanut butter sandwich if the ingredients are stored within his reach. Changing where the bread and peanut butter "live" is better than having an ambitious child climbing the cabinet so he doesn't have to ask you to make his lunch.

GIVE YOUR CHILD CHOICES

Choices are good. Every time you can give your child a choice instead of a straight command, you increase the odds of being obeyed, AND you exercise the child's decision-making skills.

It is important to remember that you should never offer a choice unless you are okay with both, or all, of the options. You do not ask, "Would you rather go to bed or stay up and watch TV?" You ask, "Are you ready to get ready for bed now and have time for a story, or do you want to play for another ten minutes then go right to bed with no story?"

Start giving your baby choices immediately. A ball or a rattle? A big cookie or two small ones? Choices for small children must be limited or they become overwhelming. When the kids are choosing their clothes to set out for the next morning, do not ask the three-year-old, "What do you want to wear tomorrow?" Limit the options and say, "Do you want to wear your red sweater, or your new blue shirt?"

You may have to emphasize, "Those are your choices. You can decide between them or I will choose for you." You would be wise to make one of the choices a garment the child usually wants to wear, whenever possible.

One of the things the child is expected to do at bedtime each night will probably be to put the clothes worn that day into a dirty clothes container of some kind. If that has not been done, his favorite garments may not be available, which provides another teaching moment.

As Suzy is wailing that she will only wear her blue pants, she should be reminded that they were not put away properly and therefore did not get washed yesterday. Remind her that there will be more washing done tomorrow, so she will have them the next day, but she will have to wear something else in the meantime. Ask her what she might have done differently in order to have them ready today. Do not lecture. She will get the point, whether she answers the question or not.

Giving choices and asking questions to encourage thinking are great ways to teach your children. These teaching methods demonstrate that you love the child, because you are taking the trouble of offering a choice instead of barking out a command.

This approach also encourages self-discipline because it provides a chance to practice waiting for whatever is wanted, and doing what it takes to get it. It develops self-sufficiency because the child is learning to take care of herself. Eventually the child can learn to use the washer and dryer, to cook, to keep the bathroom clean, and everything else you can teach them.

FEARS

It might seem that by elementary school, a child should be past fears of things like darkness or storms. Some children do outgrow such fears easily. Some, however, are just becoming aware of some of the dangers of life in the big world. Older children will notice newscasts about hurricane damage, tidal waves, earthquakes, mass shootings, or other horrible things more. They will also hear talk about such things at school. For many children, age brings maturity and the disappearance of specific fears. For others, age brings an increased sense of vulnerability and an acute awareness of how overwhelming the world can be.

Be as calm and reassuring as you can in talking about fearful events. Be honest, but reassure the child that the media shows us anything awful that happens anywhere in our world. Bad things have always been happening somewhere. We just haven't always known about all of it because most of it is far away.

A small flashlight kept beside the bed may be enough to dispel fears of things in the dark. A night-light should be left on in the child's room until he or she decides to turn it off.

HURTING OTHERS

Hurting others is not okay. When a child bites or kicks or hurts another child, he must learn that such behavior is not acceptable. He should be removed from the activity and suffer an appropriate consequence. Having to sit out of the playtime and watch others having fun may be adequate. He must learn to apologize and ask forgiveness. If he has broken a toy, he should replace it or offer a substitute. It should cost him something that matters, but don't make too big an issue of it. Sometimes, when children feel hurt by the divorce process they may behave in ways that hurt others. They may or may not justify it by saying their own world has been destroyed. It is still not OK to hurt others.

ANGER

Dealing with anger is an important element of self-management. If your child becomes angry, he or she needs a lesson in how to handle anger or frustration. Kids lose their temper, just like the rest of us. It is important to acknowledge and confirm the child's anger, and to teach him/her how to express it in acceptable ways. Here's one way you might deal with it:

- *Address the anger*: "Suzy, you look angry when you stomp your feet and your face scrunches up."

- *Acknowledge*: "It's okay to be angry."

- *Empathize*: "I get angry, too, when I can't have something I really want."

- *Problem-solve*: "You know, I'll bet you can figure out a way to solve this problem. What do you think might work?"

A child's bad mood may be very understandable. If you have Junior in Wal-Mart at 10 p.m., it's no wonder he's crabby. It's two hours past his bedtime, and you are probably not in a great mood yourself. If that has to happen, think ahead and do whatever you can to help him get through it. Give him a treat, explaining that the treat is "extra" because it's so late and you are both so tired. Sometimes, a child may not always be able to articulate why he is angry or what makes him irritable. Such displaced anger frequently emerges during or after divorce, but it still should be handled like other anger episodes.

MANIPULATION VERSUS POWER

Kids quickly learn to manipulate their parents. Recognize this and realize that manipulation is used by a child to gain power. The less power he feels he has over his own existence, the more he will try to get power in unhealthy ways.

Not all manipulation is unhealthy. A kid who uses his charms and strengths to get his way may be doing so appropriately. A week in which Suzy the teenager is unusually willing to do all her chores, does not antagonize Junior, and then asks to stay out an extra 30 minutes past regular curfew on Friday for Homecoming, is probably practicing a good skill. She has done nothing dishonest, and should be given a chance to get the reward she has been silently working toward.

A ten-year-old who goes into a rage because it is bedtime, and starts yelling and throwing things, is using negative manipulation. He is saying, "If I don't get my way, I'll make trouble for you."

Do not give in or negotiate in this situation. Tell him that you will not talk with him until he can speak calmly and quietly. Tell him so calmly and quietly yourself. Model the behavior you want him to copy. Tell him that trying to intimidate you will not get him what he wants. Do not provide an audience for his fit. Tell him you are going outside for 15 minutes until he can get himself under control. Tell him you expect him to do the right thing. Go out on the front porch, and give him 15 minutes to finish up and calm down, think about his situation, and then do the right thing.

Parents need to agree on how to handle manipulation issues, especially during and after a divorce. If Junior can play one parent against the other, he surely will. If you are handling it alone, find another like-minded parent to call for moral support at times like these.

Children Need Exercise

Children need exercise as part of a balanced life. Plenty of exercise prevents boredom, enhances a healthy lifestyle, and is a great outlet for extra energy. As we are all aware, there is a raging epidemic of childhood obesity in the United States. This is partly due to inactivity, coupled with an excess of processed foods. Another reason for children to exercise as much as possible is that studies show that inactive children become inactive adults, increasing health risks.

Children are born naturally active. It is an instinctive behavior to explore and move. They begin by rolling and then graduate to crawling, walking and running. To thrive, they need daily physical activity, for both physical and mental development. It is vital that children exercise when they are developing their bodies and minds.

Childhood is an excellent time for children to be exposed to as many types of physical activities as possible. The more fun the exercise, the better. Let your child try out swimming, soccer, gymnastics, dancing, martial arts, or any other kind of exercise that is available. Children also need some time each day for "free play" where they can run outside with friends or play unorganized sports. This is essential. It helps develop coordination and creativity, while also developing important muscle groups.

Active, healthy children need at least an hour of physical activity every day. Regular exercise does the following for your child:

- Decreases stress.

- Helps maintain a healthy weight.

- Builds healthy bones, muscles, and joints.

- Helps ensure a good night's sleep.

- Develops the kinesthetic abilities.

- Enhances self-esteem.

Exercise not only makes children healthier, it can also make them more intelligent, because it stimulates the brain as well as the body. New research shows that in addition to causing the release of "feel-good" brain chemicals called endorphins, exercise can contribute to the formation of new connections among nerve cells in the brain, and even to the growth of new cells. Other research has underscored the strong correlation between exercise and higher mental function. It appears to be true: A healthy body really does equal a healthy mind.

Congratulations! Now you have finished Lesson 5 and it's time for another quiz.

LESSON 5 QUIZ

1.   When a child is throwing a fit, ask yourself:
     a.   Why is he/she being such a brat?
     b.   Is he tired?
     c.   Is he hungry?
     d.   b and c

2.   When a child spills milk, you should:
     a.   Say, "Look at what you did!" and clean it up for him
     b.   Tell the child that it's okay, accidents happen, and clean it up for him or her
     c.   Tell the child that it's okay, that accidents happen, and help him or her clean it up
     d.   None of the above

3.   The fastest way to end a power struggle is to:
     a.   Threaten to ground the child
     b.   Threaten to embarrass her in front of her friends
     c.   Tell her that she should stop acting like a baby
     d.   Offer the child choices that you can control

4.   If your child hurts someone, you should:
     a.   Ask your child, "Are you okay?"
     b.   Spank him and put him in a time-out
     c.   Call your ex-spouse
     d.   Tell him, "I love you, but I don't love this behavior. What can we do to make the other child feel better? The first thing you must do is to say, 'I'm sorry.'"

5.   The best time to use sarcasm is:
     a.   When you are not getting through to your children
     b.   When you are in public
     c.   When you want to discipline children
     d.   Never

6.   If you have your own meltdown in front of the children, it is best to:
     a.   Tell your children you are not sorry
     b.   Tell them that it's their fault
     c.   Blame your ex-spouse
     d.   Apologize, and explain that parents have meltdowns too, and that it's not okay

7.   After your child has a meltdown it is important to:
    a.   *Tell the child he is wrong and needs to grow up and act like an adult*
    b.   *Identify the source, explain the feelings, and show the child an appropriate manner to express those feelings*
    c.   *Validate the child's feelings, explain that they are normal, but that acting out is not acceptable*
    d.   *b and c*

8.   Which of the following statements is correct?
    a.   *Children should go outside for at least three hours a day*
    b.   *Children should exercise every day because it is physically, mentally, and emotionally healthy for them*
    c.   *Couch potato syndrome is caused by eating potatoes and other starches*
    d.   *Exercise is good for your body, but it won't make you smarter*

9.   T / F   To increase cooperation, you should tell children that they will get spanked if they don't do what you tell them to do, and offer them treats for doing what you want.

10.   T / F   You should never propose a choice that you cannot allow the child to make.

LESSON 6
PARENTING TEENS

Older children who have had responsible parents for 12 years or more are ready for more responsibility and greater freedom. Because they are older, they are more able to discuss the situations they face, and should be able to see if the way the family has been functioning is letting them down. Those who have not already learned some self-control and self-sufficiency will need more basic training.

If you have serious behavioral problems with your children, call a family meeting. Before the meeting, think through all you want to do and say. Write it down. Explain, with examples, what is not working in your household. Describe what needs to happen and how you intend to see that it happens.

ESTABLISH ROUTINES

If you have not had effective routines for school mornings, after school, bedtime, and weekends, work to create your ideal routines. Let the whole family help to design the final product in the meeting.

Working together, you should be able to plan out all the things that need to be included. If something is getting overlooked, someone can say, "What about teeth brushing?" Set out new rules, consequences, rewards, and let the children discuss why each one is or is not a good idea. They may even be able to suggest some good additions.

This requires a lot of preparation on your part, but if you want the effort to succeed, you will do it. You may want to tackle this one piece at a time. Maybe just one new routine per month is all you can handle.

You must make clear at the first meeting that you are committed to keeping every promise you make. Do not agree to do anything you do not feel confident you can do. But consistency and follow-through are critical.

The children will test you, especially if they have been able to wear you down and get their way in the past. Your resolve to be faithful to the new arrangements will eventually be a wonderful example for your children of how things can change for the better.

In all training programs with your children, you should remind them that the goal is still to make them *independent, responsible, functional adults*.

COMMUNICATE

Communication with teens is possible. Really. Understand that teens will certainly not open up to anybody who criticizes them for how they feel. It is important to convey that you are a *safe person* to talk to when you deal with your teenagers. They have to trust you and feel they can safely share confidences, or they will clam up and there will be no real communication.

It's vital to teenagers that their voices be heard, and that they have an actual dialogue with their parents. Seemingly endless lectures from Dad and Mom are not as effective as a genuine give-and-take between parent and child.

This means parents have to learn to listen—really listen—to what teens have to say about how they feel and what they think. Parents have to make teens feel secure that they can bare their souls, if necessary, and the parents will not betray their confidences. Listening like this is a matter of practice. Get used to it and you'll reap the rewards.

There are a few things that are nearly guaranteed to ruin any talk with your teen. It is almost always a mistake to:

- Say, "It's none of your business" to a personal question from your teen. When she asks an honest question, she deserves a polite and equally honest answer. The answer may be something like, "That's a rather private matter, and I'd rather not talk about it." The main thing is to be at least as kind as you would be with your best friend.

- Mock him or one of his friends. That is a mean thing to do in any situation. You want to set a better example. If you don't like one of his friends, ask your child to tell you about the friend's best and worst points. Your child is getting something he wants from that relationship. It will help you to know just what that is.

- Say, "You wouldn't understand." It may be true, but that is a bad way to express it. The child has some understanding already, or would not be asking about it. You might want to ask, "How does it look to you? What would you say is going on?" That way, you have a better idea of where the child's understanding is. You might even get an insight you have missed yourself.

- Say, "I don't care what your friends are doing." What your teen's friends are doing matters a *lot* to him or her. It would be better to say, "Let's talk about this. What do you think of the choices they are making? Is there anything about those choices that bothers you?"

HANDLING MONEY

Your older children will need to learn how to handle money. How much you can put in their hands depends on your financial resources, as well as your estimation of their maturity levels. If they can take on a small after-school job, that is a good learning tool. Babysitting for a neighbor, working at a grocery store, or doing yard work are among the neighborhood opportunities often available to teens.

If your son can do yard work within walking distance of your house, you can let him use the family mower. He should buy the gas and pay for any necessary repairs. Or negotiate a loan with him to buy a used mower from Craigslist, the newspaper classifieds, or a mower shop.

A teen who earns his own money has a sense of real world power. He will also have to learn about taxes and budgets and managing personal resources. That's important, too.

Allowances are another important tool for teaching money management. Allowances should be just that, and *not* payment for doing regular chores. A child should do chores because he or she is a contributing part of the family. Extra chores or special jobs, however, might be done for cash. One child might pay another child to do his chores, but that should be negotiated between the children. Do keep an eye on any such negotiations to make sure that older kids don't take advantage of younger ones.

GROUNDING

Grounding can be an effective disciplinary tool when it is used appropriately. But first, you have to define what grounding means in your home. Set the rules. Does grounding apply to contact with friends only? Does it apply to attendance at social events? What about Internet contact and phone calls? When unacceptable behavior occurs in a group setting, like missing a curfew, do you automatically declare those friends off-limits during the grounding period?

Grounding can be effective only if it is applied at the right time, in the right circumstances, and for the right length of time. If not, it can cause a tremendous amount of friction and resentment and drive a wedge between parents and teenagers.

For children in general and for teens in particular, interaction with their peer group is a strong priority. As they mature, it is natural for them to branch out from family and connect with others of their own age. This is not to be discouraged, since after all, parents do hope the kids will grow up and move out at some point. Gradually connecting more and more with people outside the family is an important part of that transition to adulthood and independence.

As parents, and onetime teenagers ourselves, we intuitively know that these associations are important to our teens. So when discipline is called for, taking those associations away from them for a time seems to be an effective strategy. In many cases, it actually is. Fear of being grounded will often keep a teenager in line, as teens do not like being restricted in their behavior. In fact, there are few things a teen values more than having freedom of choice.

But if grounding is used inappropriately, it will usually backfire. It may just result in a teen getting sneakier and more deceptive, in order to get what he or she wants without the parents finding out. Or, as we said above, it may drive a serious, long-lasting wedge between you and your teenager. What does a parent need to do to successfully use this disciplinary tool and get the child to actually change his or her behavior?

First, avoid unreasonable consequences. Most parenting experts agree that we should work to establish natural consequences for children's behavior. The more intuitive the consequence, the more effective it will be in preventing unacceptable behavior.

For example, would a total and lengthy grounding from all social activity be an effective punishment for shoplifting? Probably not, unless the event occurred when your teen was with the wrong friends. In that case, grounding from contact with those friends outside of school, combined with another consequence like community service, or working without pay for the business from which they shoplifted, would be a more fitting consequence.

Ideally, grounding should last long enough for the bad decision the teen made to be corrected, as well as long enough to be a deterrent to future misbehavior. The attitude with which the teen accepts the parents' decision is important. An attitude of, "You're right, I did a stupid thing," is preferable to stomping off and moping for a week.

When you make your list of consequences, it is usually a good idea to build in a "time off for good behavior" clause. If Suzy flunked an English assignment because she didn't turn it in, she may have a consequence of being grounded for two weeks. However, if she talks to the teacher and gets a chance to turn in the assignment late with an automatic 10-point penalty, and does so with good results, a 50% reduction in the length of the grounding punishment might be called for. Her actions show that she has taken responsibility for the problem and taken steps to fix it. She has probably learned something important from the experience.

Of course, wrecking the family car at high speed would deserve a much stiffer punishment, because such unchecked behavior could have such dire results for her and other people.

A teen whose grades slip noticeably can reasonably have her going and coming restricted so she can spend more time studying. If her grades improve in two weeks, some of her freedom can be restored. A teacher can be contacted for weekly progress reports. Usually, a teacher will happily help a parent track a student's short-term progress when the parent has explained the plan. Better yet, the student should explain to the teacher why her parent wants a report at the end of each week.

When it comes to consequences like grounding, they are most effective when immediate, intense, and short. Lengthy grounding often runs the risk of becoming a power struggle in which the teen no longer makes a connection between his behavior and the consequences, and only attributes the grounding to "mean" or "malicious" parents.

AUTHORITY

No one likes to feel powerless. When a youngster feels he or she has no power over what's going on around him, the only way he can exercise any control is to resist. Your son may refuse to get out of bed and refuse to do his work. Your daughter may refuse to eat. He does not need to sleep all day, and she is still hungry, but the need to exercise at least a minimum of control is stronger than the other needs. These children do not lack motivation. The motivation, however, is to do something his or her way, instead of your way.

James Lehman, author of *The Total Transformation Program*, says:

> … *the child who uses resistance to control lacks both social skills and problem solving skills. It's important to define the difference between the two. Social skills are how to talk to other people, how to be friendly, how to feel comfortable inside your own skin, and how to deal with people's kindness. Problem solving skills are the skills that help kids figure out what people want from them, how to give it, how to deal with other people's behavior, expectations, and demands. Problem solving skills are needed to help a child handle being criticized in class. Many times the real reason kids don't want to do their homework is because they're simply lazy about the work or they don't want to be criticized in class and held accountable for their work. (See http://www.raisingsmallsouls.com/ motivating)*

We want to be clear about this point: everyone is motivated. The question is, motivated to do what? If a child looks like he's not motivated, you have to look at what he is accomplishing, and assume that this is what he's motivated to do. The first part of the solution is getting him to be motivated to do something else.

To assume that the child who won't get out of bed is unmotivated is an erroneous way of looking at the situation. He *is* motivated.

He's simply motivated to do nothing, because in this case, doing nothing means resisting and holding back in order to exercise control over his own existence.

It is the job of the parent to help his or her child find positive ways to solve the problem of authority. *To simply punish a teen for not obeying will not work.* You need to present clear choices. The limits must be set with well-defined consequences for crossing the line and adequate rewards for doing well. This system of teaching should have been established at a young age for each child. If it was not, adapting to it will be more difficult for an older child, but it will also be more necessary.

You should explain the choices and their consequences in detail. "If you do not do your homework and your grades reflect that, then you will have a more restricted schedule in the evenings. You will not use the computer for games, or the Wii, or watch TV from suppertime until bedtime. That schedule will continue until your grades are adequate. Once your grades are back up, you can have those privileges back, and if they stay up in the next grade period we will buy that new game you want."

Then let the young person make the choice. Do not nag or remind him or her that there is homework to do. When grades come out, be prepared to sympathize, and then follow up with the promised consequences. Those consequences need to be agreed on in advance, not imposed after the fact. If you want no report card grades under a "B" for any grading period, set that as the standard before school starts for the year. If your child wants to play sports, or to drive his or her own car, those can be the rewards for meeting minimum grade expectations.

Working out the list of consequences and rewards with you is a valuable exercise for your teen in problem solving and negotiation. Encourage your teen to work with you, and demonstrate clearly how to do this without getting emotional or overbearing. Those skills are critical to successful adult life. The best way to learn them is with loving parents.

Explain often to your young person that you want him or her to learn how to do grown-up things. Finding solutions to problems is one of the biggest. So if there is a problem that the child is solving by passive resistance, use it as an opportunity to talk through negotiation skills. Remind your child that you want to help him or her become self-sufficient. You want your teen to be ready to take over complete control of his or her own life, one step at a time.

That's it for Lesson 6! Here's another quiz.

LESSON 6 QUIZ

1.   Communication with your teen requires
      a. *A feeling of safety*
      b. *Active listening*
      c. *Genuine interest*
      d. *All of the above*

2.   T / F   Making fun of your teen can sometimes be effective in keeping him or her in line.

3.   T / F   Teaching your teen effective money management is a relatively unimportant part of parenting.

4.   T / F   "Natural consequences" is a teaching technique reserved for young children; it should not be applied to teens.

5.   T / F   The goal of grounding is to display your power and authority as a parent.

6.   T / F   Teens feel more motivated when they feel more empowered in their lives.

7.   T / F   Giving a teen choices increases a sense of power, and it also increases responsibility.

8.   T / F   It's usually best to minimize consequences so as not to alienate your children.

9.   T / F   Simply punishing a teen for not obeying is not an effective way to change behavior.

10.   T / F   To help a teen become independent, a parent should try to stay completely out of the child's life.

LESSON 7
RESOLVING CONFLICT WITH CHILDREN

Conflict is a fact of life. It occurs between parents and children, just like it occurs between adults. How you handle conflict with your children will determine the quality of your relationship with them.

If you view conflict as something that shouldn't ever happen because it harms relationships, you may try to avoid it and hope the problem will go away. Unfortunately, you will soon discover that it doesn't disappear all by itself.

However, if you see conflict as a fact of life and an opportunity to strengthen relationships, you have a way of resolving it by turning it into something creative and positive.

10 WAYS TO RESOLVE CONFLICT WITH YOUR CHILDREN

Try these simple and straightforward strategies:

1. Agree on a mutually acceptable time and place to discuss the conflict. (Make sure you show up on time.)

2. State the problem as you see it, and list your concerns.

    *   Make "I" statements, such as "I think that behavior was out of line."

    *   Avoid judgments, accusations, and absolute statements such as "always" or "never."

3. Let the child/teen have his or her say.

    *   Do not interrupt, override or contradict while your child is talking. This is a discussion, and that means both sides get to give their points of view and to state their feelings.

    *   Do not allow name-calling, put-downs, threats, obscenities, yelling, or intimidating behavior.

4.   Listen and ask questions.

   • Ask fact-based questions to make sure you understand the situation: *Who? What? Where? When? How?*

   • Ask exploratory questions: *What if? What are you saying? Is this the only solution to our problem? What if we did such and such? Are there other alternatives to this situation?*

   • Avoid accusatory "why" questions: *Why do you act like that? Why do you jump to conclusions?*

   • Acknowledge the child's feelings and perceptions, even if you don't agree with him at times. Let them express themselves as freely and openly as possible. Then, use your own words to restate what you think the child means and wants. "*Let me see if I understand what you're saying…*"

5.   Stick to one conflict at a time.

   • Do not change the subject or allow it to be changed.

   • Try saying, "I understand your concern, but I'd like to finish what we're talking about before we discuss this new issue."

6.   Seek common ground. Brainstorm answers to the conflicts that allow everyone to own at least part of the solution. There are always a number of ways to deal with a situation, and a little thought and conversation can often produce a solution that is satisfactory to both sides.

   • "What do we agree on so far?"

   • "What concerns do we share about how to resolve this?"

   • "Okay, we agree that curfew on Friday night will be 11 o'clock, instead of 10 like it is on school nights."

7.   Request behavioral changes only.

   • Don't ask kids to change their attitudes.

   • Don't ask them to "feel" differently about something.

   • If you want them to stop doing something, suggest an alternative action.

8.   Agree to the best way to resolve the conflict and to a timetable for implementing it. Who will do what, and when? Be specific about this and stick with the timeline for change.

9.   Put it in writing.

10. If the discussion breaks down, reschedule another time to meet. Consider bringing in a third party. Introducing another person, especially if he or she is neutral, often helps break a stalemate.

ALWAYS KEEP YOUR PROMISES

The first rule of parenting is to always keep your promises. In bringing a child into the world, you have implicitly promised to love and care for him or her. It is your obligation as a parent. To do less for your child would make you less than human.

Keeping your word to your child is a big way in which you show your love. If you say you will be at a soccer game to watch your child play, you must show up and be on time. Your child must always feel confident that, if you say you will do something, you will not choose to do anything else.

In the same way, if you say skipping school will get your child grounded for a month, he must be absolutely certain that you will enforce that rule. That kind of certainty provides security for a child. Your daughter must know from experience that you mean what you say. Tell her that she may go to the mall only after her room is picked up. If she fiddles around until her ride comes, she may not leave until her room is picked up. Do not listen to arguments. Enforce the rules with consistency, and do not allow yourself to be manipulated.

Now it's time for another quiz.

Lesson 7 Quiz

1. T / F Conflict must be avoided at all costs.

2. T / F In conflict resolution, you should focus on what the other person is doing wrong.

3. T / F When the child is airing his/her grievance, do not interrupt.

4. T / F Saying, "you always do this" is a really good way to start a conversation.

5. T / F "Why" questions are generally the best way to start resolving a conflict.

6. T / F When resolving conflict, stick to one topic at a time.

7. T / F Ask fact-based questions.

8. T / F Make sure you ask the child if he or she minds being wrong all the time.

9. T / F Do not allow name-calling, put-downs, threats, obscenities, yelling, or intimidating behavior.

10. T / F Never use a timetable.

LESSON 8
BEFORE YOU TELL YOUR CHILDREN

DEVELOPING PARENTING PLANS FOR DIVORCE

It comes as no surprise that children of divorcing parents usually fare best when they maintain a close relationship with both parents. Making that happen for your children needs to be your *highest priority* in working out the details of the divorce agreement.

A child of divorcing parents feels a great deal of anxiety and emotional pain when the parents continue to battle. As difficult as it may be, for the sake of your child and for your own emotional well-being, it's vital that you avoid open conflict with your spouse, or former spouse. Do not ever argue or fight in front of your children.

Remember that both of you want to do the best thing for your children. Keep that in mind and remind yourself of it often. Assuming that both of you are taking this parenting course and reading this handbook, try to discuss the Responsible Parenting goals. If you can agree that both of you want the children to feel safe and loved, and to grow to be self-disciplined and self-sufficient, you have a positive foundation on which to build.

If you are in litigation over the terms of your divorce, your attorney may be pursuing very aggressive tactics to win as much power for you in the settlement as possible. You may need to have a very honest discussion with your attorney to explain your desire for a harmonious co-parenting plan.

If your former spouse will do the same with his or her attorney, the chances are much better that a plan can be arranged that does not add to the hurt and anger already present. You are your attorney's client. In that position, you are the boss. Make sure the person working for you knows that your child's best interests are your first consideration in everything.

Keep in mind that negotiation is to be preferred over litigation. You want to develop a parenting plan with your former spouse, which will be good for your child. Instead of traditional litigation in court, mediation and negotiation can often resolve the disputes of a divorce more quickly and with less conflict.

MEDIATION

Mediation is accomplished with a third person who is emotionally neutral and trained to help divorcing couples negotiate agreements. It has been shown that parents and children are much closer over time when the parents used a mediator to settle divorce issues that involve their children.

A trained mediator can help divorcing parents learn to manage their emotions so that the grief, anger, and resulting stress do not damage the children over time. Managing those emotions is also very helpful for the well-being of the wounded parents.

A team may be assembled to help a divorcing couple reach the needed legal agreements. This approach is called collaborative practice. A collaborative practice team will include lawyers, a financial specialist, and a child specialist or coach. The child specialist is on the team to specifically be a voice for the interests of the child or children in the family.

CUSTODY AND VISITATION

Two emotionally loaded words that are usually used for parenting plans are custody and visitation. When a couple decides to end a marriage, emotions are high and conflict is almost always present. Decisions about custody of the children are difficult to make when you are feeling overwhelmed by grief, loss, and anger.

When one parent is granted *sole legal custody* of the children, he or she has the full duty and responsibility to make decisions about all aspects of the children's care. If the court decides that the parent who does not have sole legal custody still has the right to spend time with the child or children, a fixed amount of *visitation* time is set.

If *joint legal custody* is established, the parents share in making decisions about the children's health, education, and religious activities. Joint physical custody usually means the children live with each parent part of the time, but not always in equal amounts.

As parents, judges, and legal and mental health professionals have come to better understand the importance of joint custody, it is now acknowledged that having both parents active in their children's lives is vitally important to the children.

JOINT CUSTODY VARIATIONS

There are two basic kinds of joint custody: joint *legal* custody and joint *physical* custody. In some cases, parents may be given joint legal custody, and yet may not be given joint physical custody. If the divorcing parents can work together well enough to set up joint legal and physical custody, studies show that it is the best arrangement for all concerned.

Being able to work together without conflict is essential for joint custody to benefit the children.

However, when parents are jealous about establishing and protecting their own time with the child, they may become more focused on defending their rights than nurturing the emotional health of their children. The child may want desperately to be with both parents, but may get very stressed out by feeling like the ball in a tennis match. If the parents cannot control their anger and frustrations, it is best that children be protected from such conflicts.

A child should be protected from contact with a parent who is violent, abusive, or abusing substances like alcohol and drugs. In those instances, only supervised visitations should be allowed, if any.

Parents who can be respectful, flexible, and businesslike, open to all points of view, and focused on the child's best interests above everything else will be the most successful in parenting through divorce. However, this is a high ideal, and for some it can be very tough to achieve. You may be wise to consult a specially trained mediator, lawyer, or mental health professional to help the two of you work out a parenting plan between you.

Divorcing parents who can agree to joint custody arrangements may want to think of it as "shared residence" rather than "joint custody". Sharing anything with your former spouse may be painful to even consider. But unless the other parent is dangerous to you or your children, you must do it for your children simply because it is in their best interests. Remember, that is your first priority during the divorce process.

Joint custody arrangements may follow the *Parallel Parenting* model, or the *Cooperative Parenting* model. It is also possible to use a combination of the two plans.

PARALLEL PARENTING

Parallel Parenting is an arrangement for parenting that keeps contact between the former spouses to a minimum. Each parent is responsible for parenting while in charge of the child. Parenting plans are agreed on in detail and followed by each parent. When changes are needed, they are negotiated in a businesslike manner. The children are transferred from one parent to the other at school, or at an emotionally neutral site like a park or mall.

COOPERATIVE PARENTING

Cooperative Parenting can be used when the parents can be pleasant in each other's presence. One parent can visit the other's residence to pick up or drop off the child. Changes to schedules or other parenting decisions can be arranged in a brief, polite phone call. The more cooperative a parenting plan can be, the better the child's relationship will be with the non-resident parent.

Either type of plan will work for the children, so long as conflict is kept to a minimum, and both parents use responsible parenting methods in their homes. The children must not feel that it is going to upset one parent to mention the other one. The child must not have to build separate emotional boxes for each parent, constantly moving from one to the other and trying to live two separate lives. Avoiding such a situation must be your goal in making custody decisions.

In the early stages of divorce, emotions are usually very strong. Minimizing contact with your former partner may be the only way for you to get through the early phases. Give yourself all the buffer you need, holding onto the hope that a more cooperative relationship may be possible in a few months, or even a year or two.

Give yourself a pep talk, reminding how much you want to make things easier for your child or children. Ask, by phone or email, if you and your divorcing partner can discuss what will be best for the children. Ask to agree that you will avoid talking about anything else. Suggest a list of things on which you need to agree. These suggestions are probably best made in writing, so if you can arrange this agreement by email, that may be a good option.

When communicating, try to use "I" statements rather than "You" statements. Try to think of your soon-to-be "ex" as the co-parent of your children, instead of the former spouse whom you may dislike intensely at present. *Your goal is to take care of your children.* You need to both agree on that goal, and keep reminding yourself of it. You may have to say, "I'm trying to keep the children's best interests in mind here," but don't say, "You promised to keep the children's best interests in mind!" Accusations and criticism are not constructive.

If you can do it without criticizing one another, try to agree on ways that each of you can reinforce the goals of the plan. If each of you can identify at least one way in which you can do a better job of parenting, it will demonstrate your good faith. Do not suggest ways in which the other co-parent should improve. That is neither your job, nor within your control any more.

Do not say, "You've got to stop letting Junior run all over you." Instead say, "I will set firm rules and stick to them. I'll also let you know what those rules are. If you think they are not good for Junior, let's talk about it. If you can hold him to the same rules, he will be the better for it. He's going to need consistency."

It is critical that you, as divorced or separated parents, do not send messages back and forth through the child. Do not say, "I wish you would tell your father to be on time." Do not say, "You've got to get your mother to follow our agreement about sending your homework with you." Do not criticize your former spouse in front of your children. If you can't say something nice, just say nothing at all. Your child must not be made to feel like a bone being fought over by two dogs.

The list of things you need to work out should cover custody arrangements, housing, schedules, finances, distribution of pets, and other things that will come up as you go. Start with the obvious items and work through each thing you and your former partner think of. Consider things carefully. Do not make snap judgments. Try to make suggestions and not demands. Listen carefully to the reasoning behind your co-parent's suggestions.

Agree, if you can, that nothing is yet written in stone. You want to remain as flexible as possible. Remember, things change. What is best for the children right now may shift as the months go by.

The age of your child or children at present is a critical factor. One parent may not be able to stay home with a very young child, while the other is. As the child gets older, he or she will more easily be able to spend more time with the working parent. That should be acknowledged from the start. Whatever you decide, your child will be healthier emotionally in the long run if he or she can spend time with each parent in a nurturing, loving environment.

Circumstances for you and the co-parent will also shift. You want to set an example of being as cooperative as possible. You might even find that you and the other parent can work together better than you were able to live together. Remember, too, that you may need cooperation from the co-parent later, so try not to poison your own well.

Some questions that should be on your list when negotiating agreements:

- Who will stay in your current residence?

- Where will the other spouse live?

- When will the children be with each parent?

- Who will take the children to team practices, music lessons, and other activities?

- How will unexpected changes in plans and schedules be handled? It's best to have a procedure in place before inevitable changes pop up.

- What is the best way for the children to contact each of you?

- Which one of you should be listed first on the emergency contact list for school, sports, and other activities?

You do not have to decide everything immediately, but you do want to keep working on it. Do try to be civil at all times and gracious whenever you can. Agree to avoid discussion of any of the background causes of your divorce. That is not in the best interest of the children.

In some cases, the parent who has moved out may be able to come to the other parent's home for an hour or two for feeding time or bath time. If both parents can be comfortable with that arrangement, the residential parent can take a break from full responsibility and catch a much-needed break. A baby might live full-time with his mother, but as the infant grows, he or she can go out with Dad for outings or for an overnight at his home. Eventually the parenting arrangement may change so that the child can stay with Dad on the weekends, or move between homes on some other schedule. Remember to stay flexible and keep the child's emotional best interests in mind.

This assumes that both parents are responsible, caring, stable adults. Issues such as abuse, some kinds of mental illness, or substance dependency can drastically change parenting plans. The children's well-being must always be the top priority.

Now you have finished a very important lesson in responsible parenting. Test your understanding with another quiz.

LESSON 8 QUIZ

1. When negotiating a plan for your child's care, remember that
   a. *Whatever you agree on cannot be changed*
   b. *You need to discuss the reasons for the divorce*
   c. *The plan may shift over time and as the child grows*
   d. *You should be honest about what you think the other parent is doing wrong*

2. Parallel parenting and Cooperative parenting are different styles of
   a. *Visitation*
   b. *Joint physical custody*
   c. *Joint legal custody*
   d. *Sole legal custody*

3. Questions that must be addressed in your co-parenting agreement include:
   a. *Where will each parent live?*
   b. *Who will take the child to music lessons and team practices?*
   c. *How will you handle schedule changes and emergencies?*
   d. *All of the above*

4. T / F   Children of divorcing parents do best when they keep a close relationship with both parents.

5. T / F   Both parents should strive to agree on *Responsible Parenting Goals*.

6. T / F   A trained mediator can only help with legal matters; they cannot help divorcing parents learn to manage their emotions.

7. T / F   You should examine your own emotionally charged reactions to issues of *custody* and *visitation*.

8. T / F   The child should always live primarily with the mother.

9. T / F   The best way to communicate with your ex-spouse is to send messages through your child.

10. T / F   In cases where there are abuse or substance dependency issues, the child's well-being must take priority over the parent's visitation rights.

LESSON 9
TELLING YOUR CHILDREN

Now that you have made a custodial plan and drawn up responsibilities and conditions of your custodial arrangements with your spouse or ex-spouse, you need to discuss the divorce and these plans with your children. Here are some steps to take to make sure this critical discussion is successful:

1. Meet on a day when the children are not in school, and make sure you schedule plenty of time to answer questions, discuss proposed changes, and talk about worries and feelings.

2. Tailor your discussion to the child's age, emotional maturity, and disposition. Not all kids are capable of understanding the concept of divorce, but may grasp the idea of Mommy and Daddy living in different places. Some will not be interested in the details of the plan, and others will want to help with planning.

3. Tell them about the divorce together, if at all possible. This is an opportunity to let them know, first and foremost, that you love them, that you always will, and to demonstrate that as a family, you're going to meet their needs and answer their questions. Discussing things together sends an important message to your kids that you're both still capable of working together for their benefit.

4. Tell all your children at one time. It's very important that each child hears this news directly from the parents, not from a sibling or other relative who heard it first. If your children vary significantly in age, plan to share the basic information at the first meeting, and then follow up in more detail with the older children in a separate conversation.

5. A general statement should be made about the parents having grown-up problems they have not been able to resolve. Both parents should support the decision to divorce as the best thing to do. They should let the children react and answer their concerns.

6. Timing is important. Telling a three-year-old that they will be moving in a couple of months has no real meaning to them. At the same time, do not tell

them at the last minute. Discuss the near-term items thoroughly, and then talk about other changes as they approach.

7. Prepare a clear and easy-to-understand schedule and mark it on calendars for each child and each parent. One calendar blocked off with different background colors for each parent may make the schedule clearer. Write in any significant activities for the day.

8. If your spouse is unwilling or unable to attend the family meeting, follow your own plan, making sure you have included all of the relevant issues.

9. If older children stomp off and refuse to talk about it, another meeting should be set soon for further discussion. Tell your children that you want their input about the plans. Giving them a little control helps to provide a sense of security, which can be severely threatened when the family is breaking up.

10. Be prepared to handle the children's fears and emotional reactions. Assure them that the divorce is not their fault. Promise them that they will be taken care of and not abandoned. Let them know that you both still love them, and that while things will be different, they are still your children and you are still their parents.

You have completed another short, but very important lesson in responsible parenting. It is time for another quiz.

LESSON 9 QUIZ

1.   T / F   If at all possible, tell the children about the divorce together with the whole family present.

2.   T / F   It's less threatening for children to hear the news about the divorce indirectly, perhaps from a friend, older sibling, or relative, rather than directly from both parents.

3.   T / F   Prepare a clear and easy-to-understand schedule for time with Mom and time with Dad.

4.   T / F   There is much about this process that you cannot control, but the more collaborative planning in advance of telling your children the better.

5.   T / F   You should always tell your children the exact reasons you are divorcing.

6.   T / F   The timing of your announcement about the divorce to your children isn't that important.

7.   T / F   Young children may not really understand what divorce is.

8.   T / F   If your spouse won't participate in the family meeting, you can tell your children the divorce is your spouse's fault.

9.   If your child doesn't want to talk about the divorce plans, you should
   a.   *Tell him that he has to face facts*
   b.   *Ask him to help with planning*
   c.   *Point out that he is making a stressful situation worse*
   d.   *All of the above*

10.   When they hear about their parents' divorce, children may become worried that
   a.   *The divorce is their fault*
   b.   *They will be abandoned*
   c.   *Their parents don't love them anymore*
   d.   *All of the above*

LESSON 10
PARENTING IN DIVORCE

Your parenting skills, emotional strength, and personal commitment to your children are rarely tested more severely than when shepherding your children through a divorce. The rest of this handbook will deal with this dilemma.

A divorce is a kind of death. It marks the end of a relationship, the end of certain hopes and dreams of happiness. Like a death, it causes grief. The suffering is both physical and emotional. The former partners of the failed marriage have many things to be sad about. The children of those partners have to deal with grief, as well.

It is important to remember that most people experience embarrassment, guilt, and even shame when they divorce, for many reasons. They may feel:

- Worry that other people may think they didn't try hard enough

- Embarrassment because they are the topic of gossip

- Guilt that they've let their children down

- A sense of shame at being the cause of the divorce

- Worry that their children will be treated differently by other children

- Concern that their children will be forever emotionally damaged by the divorce

Do not allow those emotions to keep you from moving forward with your life. The "Serenity Prayer" that Alcoholics Anonymous has made famous may be a good motto for you to follow: seek *the serenity to accept the things I cannot change, the courage to change the things I can, and the wisdom to know the difference.*

THE GRIEF PROCESS

Studies of death and grief have identified five common stages of the process of grief. These apply to the experience of divorce as much as to the experience of death or other losses. Not every grieving person experiences all five, or in this particular order, but most people will recognize at least two of them in their own process of grief.

1. ***Denial***: There is often an "unreal" feeling, a sense that "this can't be really happening." You may think your spouse will change his or her mind. However, if papers have been filed and a judge is involved, you should assume that this time, it's for real. You will have to adjust to the new reality.

    A child may outright deny that you are divorcing, or may retreat to fantasy day-dreams.

2. ***Anger***: Your anger may be completely justified. You may have been treated very badly. You have certainly been hurt, at least emotionally. You may feel very bitter. Acknowledge and accept the anger, but avoid making any harmful actions resulting from that anger. Look for help from friends, counselors, or clergy.

    Your child may also be angry that his or her world has been crushed.

3. ***Bargaining***: You may be tempted to try to "buy back" the relationship. You may want to say, "I'll change if you will stay." Or you may accept blame for things that are not your fault. These are not the smart things to do, but this is a normal reaction to have. Admit to yourself that you feel like doing this, but do not do it. It will not work out.

    Your children, likewise, may engage in bargaining behaviors with you and your ex-spouse in an effort to prevent the divorce.

4. ***Depression***: The feeling that the world is coming to an end and you are helpless to stop it is nearly unbearable. It may seem to last forever. You may feel worthless and hopeless. Talking with a wise friend, a doctor, or someone who has been through the experience themselves is a very good thing to do. You will get through it. You may need help to do so, though, and you should accept that possibility.

    You may find that your child has withdrawn from you (or perhaps both of you). He or she may retreat into a depressive shell.

5. ***Acceptance***: Eventually reality sinks in. Talking through your problems with a friend who has been through it may help you see that the world has changed, but not ended. You need someone who understands your situation, someone who can sympathize, and help you make a plan for moving forward. Create a realistic strategy with goals and a timetable. Be patient with yourself and with your children.

    Acceptance (without resentment) is the eventual goal for your children as well.

STRESS

Many other feelings accompany the grief that comes with divorce. Sorrow, anger, loneliness, sadness, shame, anxiety and guilt often accompany serious losses. Having so many strong feelings can be very stressful, especially when accompanied by all of the other stresses of divorce.

No one has a "great" divorce. Most are close to devastating, especially when children are involved. You can, though, with acceptance and awareness, create a healthier and more peaceful environment for all parties involved.

We experience stress when we are worried, afraid, angry, or "stirred up." Stress symptoms commonly include a state of alarm and adrenaline production, resulting in exhaustion, irritability, muscular tension, and inability to concentrate. It can also produce a variety of physiological reactions, including headaches, sweating, stomachaches and elevated heart rates.

The long-term consequences of extended, unrelieved stress are devastating to our bodies. Our immune systems are not equipped to handle relentless stress. Under continuing stress, an organism begins to break down, and cardiovascular damage occurs. Many divorcing people suffer from cardiovascular problems, ulcers, stomach ailments, muscle aches, and other physical issues.

It is important to keep in mind that children experience stress in much the same way as adults do. Ongoing stress, tension, arguments, or silent wars will literally cause you and your children to become run down. You will all suffer physically, mentally, and emotionally. When a young child witnesses arguments, hostility or anger, they fear that their whole world is about to collapse. The resulting stress reaction can show up in the form of headaches, tummy aches, sleep disturbances, and behavioral problems.

You can help your children by making a conscious effort to minimize conflict and tension. Here are seven ways to lessen the stress of divorce on your children:

SEVEN WAYS TO LESSEN STRESS ON CHILDREN DURING DIVORCE:

1. ***Remove conflict.*** Keep kids out of the firing line. Don't let them hear your arguments. To the best of your abilities, keep it all positive. Just remember that they will still sense that things in the family are not the same any more.

2. ***Take a businesslike approach.*** Try to think of your exchanges with your former partner as a business deal. In business, you adopt a high degree of emotional

distance and try to stick to the topic under discussion. That approach is very useful for dealing with your spouse or ex-spouse.

3. ***Reduce change.*** Try to keep your children's lives as stable as possible during this jarring time. The less change, the better. A child's emotional stability depends upon structure in their lives, and the more things are reliable and predictable, the better.

4. ***Make quality time.*** One-on-one quality time with each child is essential. This is when they need you on a personal level more than ever. If you have several children, remember that they are all different people, and need individual "face-time" to feel loved and cherished.

5. ***Provide reassurance.*** The divorce is not their fault. Tell them everything will work out okay, even if it is different. Mommy and Daddy still love them, and always will.

6. ***Name the feelings.*** Ask them what they're feeling during the big shake-up. Guilt? Insecurity? Fear? What else? For young children with a limited vocabulary, ask them to draw pictures of how they feel.

7. ***Talk about it.*** Grieving over a family breakup is normal. Invite conversation. Help your children put their thoughts and feelings into words. Opening up reduces stress all around.

ADJUSTMENT TAKES TIME

Realize that each child's adjustment could take some time. This is a traumatic period in their lives, whether they show it or not. Some emotional and behavioral reactions to the stress of divorce may last for months or even years. Other reactions are fleeting, and last only until the situation stabilizes and the child's routine is re-established.

However long they may last, though, negative responses do not necessarily indicate permanent problems. Kids' emotional problems following divorce are usually temporary, if handled with sensitivity. Be attentive to the signs your children send about their feelings during this period, and you can help them cope more effectively with how they feel.

Grief and stress are heavy topics. This lesson's quiz may help clarify your thinking about this issue.

LESSON 10 QUIZ

1. Which of the following is not part of the grieving process?
   a. *Acceptance*
   b. *Bargaining*
   c. *Depression*
   d. *Irritation*

2. Of the stages of grief, which of the following is true?
   a. *Each phase of grief must be experienced in a specific order*
   b. *All people go through every stage of grief*
   c. *You will go through at least two stages of grief*
   d. *Lots of exercise can help you avoid grieving*

3. Divorce is like a death because:
   a. *You want to bury your ex*
   b. *You experience the loss of what could have been*
   c. *You experience a physical and emotional loss*
   d. *b and c*

4. The bargaining phase:
   a. *Is where you say, "This isn't really happening!"*
   b. *Is not part of the five stages of grief*
   c. *Causes depression*
   d. *May cause you to say, "I will change if you stay."*

5. Acceptance:
   a. *Comes at three months*
   b. *Is not necessary to move on*
   c. *Is the final phase of grief*
   d. *Means you are a wimp*

6. Stress:
   a. *May produce exhaustion*
   b. *May produce irritability*
   c. *May make it hard to concentrate*
   d. *All of the above*

7. Chronic stress:
   a. *Is good for your body*
   b. *Can make you ready for a new relationship*
   c. *Is the healthiest way to lose weight*
   d. *Can cause you to become run-down*

8. When children undergo prolonged stress:
   a. *They may get tummy aches and headaches*
   b. *They sometimes act out*
   c. *They can suffer sleep disturbances*
   d. *All of the above*

9. T / F One-on-one time with a child can help reduce the child's stress.

10. T / F When children witness arguments, hostility, and anger between their parents, they might feel that the world is collapsing around them.

LESSON 11
DEALING WITH YOUR CHILD'S ANXIETY

Anxiety is one of the most common causes of stress. What form does your anxiety take? Do you suffer from shakiness, indecisiveness, panic attacks, depression? Chances are, if you're divorcing, you're not sleeping or eating well, your mind is wandering and racing, and you feel rather overwhelmed. The truth is that many individuals going through a divorce suffer from anxiety, stress, depression, anger and other related emotions. Divorces are among the most stressful events that anyone experiences in a lifetime.

It should be encouraging to know that there are healthy ways to deal with anxiety. As advice columnist Carolyn Hax says, "Anytime you feel stuck, sort the reasons into two piles: constants, and choices. Then remind yourself as often as necessary that every choice can be changed."

When it comes to a divorce situation, most people have a lengthy list of financial worries or considerations. They also have difficulty prioritizing, frequently spending energy stressing over things they cannot control. Some things (for example, mortgage rates, the economy, the stock market, money you've already spent) you can't do anything about. Try not to worry anymore about it. Focus on what you can control now.

Major studies have shown that people's stress levels drop when they feel they have some control over the stressor. So how do you gain control?

FOCUS ON SOLUTIONS AND TAKE ACTION

Our stress levels drop when we take action. It's that simple. In order to take action, though, you have to figure out solutions that will help you move toward your goal. Even if the steps are small and incremental, each bit of progress will reduce your anxiety. Focus on the things that you can control. By taking control and taking action, you will eliminate problems and reduce your anxiety.

Write out a plan that you can start working on immediately. Figure out your priorities. Determine what issues you cannot control, and resolve not to worry about them. Prioritize other items on the list and decide what you need to address first. In another category, list items to be addressed after the top-priority issues.

This is a very important skill which must be practiced regularly. It can't be left to just thinking about it, and making a list by itself won't do any good. It requires full involvement and follow-through. Any progress will help contribute to your stability and decrease your stress, leaving you more able to tackle other problems.

ROUTINES ARE ESSENTIAL TO A SUCCESSFUL HOME LIFE

Routines help provide security to children. If you have not already had chore lists and regular times for meals, homework, and bedtime, you must create them now.

During times of upheaval such as a divorce, the stability of a routine is very important. However, routines will probably need to change, because the situation has changed. Planning new routines, or adjusting the old ones, will still improve the sense of security, and can help take stress off your already frazzled minds. You can go so far as making out menus for the week and posting them on the fridge. An older child can take responsibility for setting out the ingredients for a meal, a younger one can take charge of setting the table.

Getting everyone into new habits like this may be difficult. Set the routine up clearly, and plan for a nice reward at the end of the week to add incentive. It can be comforting to see the family working together, especially if things have been rocky for some time.

WHAT YOUR CHILDREN NEED TO KNOW ABOUT YOUR DIVORCE

Most children relate to the news of a divorce primarily in terms of how it will affect them. They need to know the immediate ramifications, and their initial reactions can range from very upset, to stoic, to relieved.

Children often believe they are the cause of the divorce. A child who wets the bed may hear his parents arguing about who will get up and help him get dry clothes. He concludes that if he didn't wet the bed, his parents would not fight and they would stay married. Another child who hears his parents arguing about her best interests may not understand

any part of the argument except her name, and conclude that she must be the reason they are angry with each other.

When you talk about the divorce with your children, you will not want to give them too much information, but they must be constantly reassured that the divorce is not their fault, and that both parents love them. It may help to point out that they have been the best part of the marriage.

Some children, wanting to be good kids, hide or disguise their distress. Some are in shock, while others exhibit delayed reactions of various kinds. Just like you, children need time to process their grief and mourn.

Your child's first reaction may actually be to try to protect you. If your child is acting like everything's okay, he or she is probably pretending so that you will not have something else to worry about. Trying to protect a parent, especially one who is obviously upset and sad, is a fairly common reaction in children. Even pre-school age children may act this way.

It is a terrible burden on them, and is not what you want your children to do. They do not have to pretend. You need to protect them, not the other way around. You can admit to them that you are sad right now, or angry, or whatever name you can give your own feelings. You want the child to be able to say how he or she is feeling, also.

Something else you can do is to pay special attention to your child. For the younger child, getting books from the library about divorce and reading them together is a good idea. As you read a page, stop and ask what your child thinks the characters are thinking. Then be quiet and listen to your child. When he or she responds, ask if that is something he or she has also felt.

Holding your child close while you talk together will give a clear reassurance that you will be supportive of him/her while you work through this difficult time.

Anger is a common reaction. In particular, studies show that boys with custodial mothers show anger more often than other children. Also, teens, whose lives might already be somewhat difficult and confusing, may well be angry that their lives have been disrupted. They might argue against the divorce, saying things like, "You always tell me to get along with people and work problems out. Why can't the two of you get along? Why can't you work it out?"

The older child will also have concerns about how others talk about his or her parents,

and how his or her friends will view the situation. A teen is often very self-conscious. Having the spotlight focused on his or her parents and their problems is not a comfortable situation for a teen.

Any child may try to manipulate his or her parents. The older child may be especially good at manipulation, but even very young children may try to manipulate the situation. Do not let your child shift a discussion of her failure to meet a behavioral requirement to a discussion of your failure to keep marriage vows. Even if it's true, it is not relevant to her behavior. As much as you would like to present an example of perfect behavior, you cannot. You are living the consequences of any mistakes you have made. You child must take the consequences of any mistake he or she makes.

When divorce enters the picture, it brings a whole new set of fears. Many children feel neglected by their parents in the divorce process. The parents are dealing with many problems, and with their own anxiety and stress. They usually do not mean to ignore the children, but their attention is frequently scattered and it does happen.

The emotional distress of divorce often shows up in the form of physical distress as well. Headaches and stomachaches in children are frequent. Nightmares and general sleeping problems are common. The best cure for these and other signs of anxiety is reinforcing stability and security. Talking about the fears of the children can be helpful, if the child wants to talk. You may need to reassure your children often that while you may be upset, you can handle it and will always be ready to hear what they think and feel about the situation.

OTHER SYMPTOMS OF TURMOIL

Other external symptoms of the turmoil in your child's emotions may include:

- Crying
- Withdrawal
- Tantrums
- Sadness
- Irritability
- Separation anxiety

Perhaps the most crucial reaction from children involves their need for continued parental presence. The children of divorce desperately need to know that the split between the parents does not mean a divide will open up between the parents and the child. You cannot just tell Junior and Suzy that you will always love him and always love her. You must show them your care, by actively listening when they talk to you, by encouraging them to talk, and by spending time with them doing "ordinary" things when they are not ready to talk about the divorce.

The parent who does not have the primary responsibility for day-to-day care of the children still has the responsibility of continuing to be supportive and authoritative. That means that if the child is going to live with Mom "most of the time," then Dad needs to make an extra effort to be in touch with the child regularly and frequently. Dad also needs to continue to support the rules Mom is using for teaching the child self-discipline. Consistency is important. A parent who lets an angry child manipulate him or her into relaxing the rules and skipping over consequences is not helping the child to grow, and is actually increasing the sense of chaos in the child's life.

CHILDREN'S WANTS AND NEEDS

The University of Missouri published the following compilation of children's wants and needs during a divorce.

WHAT I REQUIRE FROM MY MOM AND DAD:

- I need both of you to stay involved in my life. Please write letters, make phone calls, and ask me lots of questions. When you don't stay involved, I feel like I'm not important and that you don't really love me.

- Please stop fighting and work hard to get along with each other. Try to agree on matters related to me. When you fight about me, I think that I did something wrong and I feel guilty.

- I want to love you both and enjoy the time that I spend with each of you. Please look for ways to meet my needs during the time that I spend with each of you. If you act jealous or upset, I feel like I need to take sides and love one parent more than the other.

- Please communicate directly with my other parent so that I don't have to carry messages back and forth.

- When talking about my other parent, please say only nice things, or don't say anything at all. When you say mean, unkind things about my other parent, I feel like you are expecting me to take your side.

- Please remember that I want both of you to be a part of my life. I count on my mom and dad to raise me, to teach me what is important, and to help me when I have problems.

This list of wants and needs provides a very valuable insight into the child's perspective. It might well be worthwhile to type them on a sheet of paper and carry them with you so you can refer to them easily, especially just before you are about to spend time with your child.

As a child sees the family unit coming apart, he or she may fear that the parents will stop loving him just like they have stopped loving each other. The parents know that is not true, but they need to remind the child of it.

A child needs to be told that adults' love for each other is different from a parent's love of his or her child. The love of a parent for a child is born in us and never goes away, no matter what.

Remember—and remind yourself and your child—that all feelings are okay, but all behaviors are not. Feelings may be painful, but they are not "bad" like some behaviors can be.

NAMING FEELINGS

It is very important to find words to express feelings. Feelings that hurt need to be named. Naming and expressing the feelings will make them less scary and overwhelming. This is important for you, and very important for your children.

You have a more extensive vocabulary and a lifetime of experience to call on to put a name on your feelings. Helping your child name his or her painful feelings gives them some control over the feelings. Some of the feelings may be best expressed as drawings, especially for very young children. As one youngster said, "It seems like the bad feelings have to come out first before the good ones can come in."

Reading together child-oriented books about divorce can enhance your child's ability to find words describing his or her experience. Joint reading also underscores that your child is not the only one with this experience.

When a child's behavior indicates painful feelings, you should calmly observe, "Sounds as if you're feeling pretty bad right now. What could we do about how things are going that could make it a little better?" Then listen carefully.

The child's idea of what would help may be impossibility. If so, gently remind him that it is not something you can do. Then make another suggestion. If your child is feeling abandoned and upset, you might offer to shift your schedule so you can pick him up from basketball practice and have some quality time together. It may not hit the mark perfectly, but it lets your child know that you care, and that you are willing to change things when it might help.

ADAPTING TO A NEW LIFE

One of the first results of the divorce will be a new shape to the family. Mom or Dad will be moving out, if that has not already happened. As a result of the divorce, there may be a new home to get used to, and new people.

If the children are going to have to move as well, it will add extra pain and grief to the load they will already carry. If at all possible, consider arranging things so that the children can remain where they are for a year or two at least. That will give them time to begin to adjust to the new reality of their already fractured lives.

If you can assure them that they will still go to bed most nights in the room they are used to, that will be a positive thing. They may be able to look on their visits to the parent who is relocating as a special time and not a threat.

Be aware that the new residence of the departing parent may not be received well if it will be shared immediately with a new step-parent and step-siblings. Be prepared for objections from the children about having to live among strangers. It can be very uncomfortable for them.

As new family structures emerge, children will often try to play one of you against the other. That has probably happened even before the divorce, with Junior going to Mom if Dad said, "No" or vice versa. Make sure that you do not give in to this kind of manipulation.

HOLIDAYS AND VACATIONS

Holidays present a special challenge. Be sure you *do not* choose a holiday, vacation, or birthday on which to tell the children about the divorce. If you do this, you will have loaded that special time with painful memories for the rest of their lives, and possibly ruined the holiday for them forever. For the rest of your life, too, the return of that holiday will mean memories of that awful time.

Holidays will be enough of a challenge. Your family unit, before the divorce, probably had some established holiday traditions. Now you and your children's other parent will need to work out who is where on Thanksgiving, for birthdays, for other special days. Decide who will travel and how long who will stay where.

The holiday season can become complicated. If you will have the children "for Christmas," does that start at noon on Christmas Eve and end on the morning of Dec. 26? Will the children spend the first week of Christmas vacation with you and the second week with the other parent? Who gets Christmas morning? Which grandparents will get to see the children this year? When will the other family get a visit?

Summer vacation time will require juggling work schedules and travel arrangements. If the parents do not live near each other, all the sharing of time between the parents is made more complicated by travel and time considerations.

Holidays are very important to children, and parents need to be particularly sensitive to children's needs during holidays and vacations.

The following quiz will help reinforce your thoughts about *anxiety, routine*, and the value of *choices* for your children.

LESSON 11 QUIZ

1.   T / F   You can reduce anxiety by making a conscious effort to list your concerns in three categories: things you cannot control, matters that are high priority to deal with, and issues to address after those.

2.   T / F   Making a list will make a significant difference in your anxiety levels, even if you don't get around to doing anything with it.

3.   T / F   Routines for getting things done at home are fine, but they don't make much difference for children's sense of security.

4.   T / F   Getting everyone into new routines may be necessary because of divorce, but since the rules are new they will not help things feel more stable.

5.   T / F   If your child does not seem to be upset about the divorce, it is safe to assume that they are fine.

6.   T / F   Nightmares, sleeping problems, tantrums and irritability are common symptoms of be emotional stress divorce induces in children.

7.   T / F   It is critical to avoid making the child feel like they need to choose sides.

8.   T / F   Naming and expressing the feelings they are experiencing will only reinforce children's fears, and should be avoided.

9.   T / F   If the child has to move, it will add to the stress, grief and pain they experience in the divorce process. It is best to let them stay in the same place for a year or two if possible.

10.   T / F   Holidays are the best time to tell children about the divorce, because the family is all together and feeling relaxed.

LESSON 12
FINANCIAL RESPONSIBILITIES OF PARENTING

A divorce usually presents financial problems. Whatever the income level was for the couple before divorce, it must now sustain two households, as well as the expenses of the divorce itself. It may require a new or additional job for one parent, making that parent less available to the children.

Most parents love their children and provide adequate care to them. Sadly, though, some parents don't meet their needs. Failing to provide for a child's basic needs is unlawful. Proper care, as defined by the law, is providing adequate food, shelter, clothing, supervision and medical care.

The costs associated with parenting during a divorce can be mind-boggling. From paying attorney's fees and court costs to establishing new households, the burden can seem unmanageable. Below we will briefly cover some of the financial issues you may be facing, and present basic information on how to deal with them.

BANKRUPTCY

Many divorcees opt to file for bankruptcy in the aftermath of a divorce. It is important to understand that filing does not necessarily shelter you from all debts you have incurred. Should you decide to file for bankruptcy, consult an attorney first to find out what your legal situation will be. If you file, remember that your credit will be jeopardized for 10 years, which can make it difficult, if not impossible, to receive credit for low-interest loans.

TAXES

Be sure to ask your accountant, tax advisor, and/or attorney about the tax implications of divorce. For instance, some couples find that it makes more financial sense to remain legally separated for years instead of divorcing, because taxes can be higher for individuals than for married couples.

YOUR LEGAL DUTY: CHILD SUPPORT

You have a legal duty to care for your children until they reach the age of 18, get married, enter the armed forces, or until another court-ordered agreement is reached.

The amount of child support is calculated by each state differently. Statutes governing support are based upon parental income after tax has been deducted. The custodial parent—the one the child lives with—must maintain a home and meet the child's health, educational, social, and general well-being. Usually, the other parent contributes financially to the child's upbringing.

If you are paying child support, it is important to note that your parental duties do NOT end when you write a check each month. What's more, you MUST continue to pay child support, even when you do not have access to your child.

Furthermore, a stepparent's income cannot be considered when estimating child support. Only income from a parent or guardian may be considered. Again, it is important to consult an accountant and/or attorney about these issues.

Other financial issues worth noting:

- The manner in which the custodial parent chooses to spend child support dollars is within his or her discretion.

- Even when a custodial parent earns more than a non-custodial parent, payments must still be made.

- Child support is not taxable.

- Never discuss late child support payments with your children. It only upsets them.

- Wage garnishment is available in most states. Check with your attorney or state attorney general's office if you are having trouble receiving your payments on time.

- Studies have shown that parents who maintain close regular contact with their children are more apt to pay child support payments on time and regularly. This means that it will benefit you to involve your ex-spouse in your children's lives.

That is all for Chapter 12. You're almost finished!

LESSON 12 QUIZ

1.   T / F   Divorce usually simplifies finances for the whole family.

2.   T / F   Filing for bankruptcy after the divorce will protect you from all your debts.

3.   T / F   It may make more financial sense to legally separate and continue to file taxes as a married couple, because taxes can be higher for individuals.

4.   T / F   The amount of child support a parent must pay is calculated uniformly nationwide.

5.   T / F   The custodial parent is solely responsible for the child's financial needs if the custodial parent earns more than the non-custodial parent.

6.   T / F   Child support income is not taxable.

7.   T / F   The custodial parent who receives child support payments can spend that money as they think best.

8.   T / F   The income of stepparents is always factored in when calculating child support payments.

9.   T / F   A parent does not have to pay child support if he/she does not have access to the child.

10.   T / F   Parents who maintain close and regular contact with their children are more likely to make child support payments on time.

LESSON 13
FAMILY VIOLENCE

WHAT IS FAMILY VIOLENCE?

Actual language in statutes may vary from state to state, but most states follow approximately the same process, so we will use the State of Texas as an example. Family violence is defined in Chapter 5 of the Texas Code of Criminal Procedure as: (1) an act of or threat to cause physical harm by one member of a family or household against another; (2) abuse of a child by a member of the child's family or household; and (3) dating violence.

WHO CAN HELP FAMILY VIOLENCE VICTIMS?

Victims of family violence are entitled to the maximum protection from harm or abuse, or the threat of harm or abuse, as permitted by law. Family violence victims should contact their local law enforcement agencies, prosecutor, or family violence centers for assistance.

WHAT IS A PROTECTIVE ORDER?

A protective order is a civil court order issued to prevent continuing acts of family violence. The order can prohibit an offender from: (1) committing further acts of family violence; (2) harassing or threatening the victim (directly or indirectly); and (3) going to or near a school or day-care center attended by a child protected by the order.

HOW CAN A FAMILY VIOLENCE VICTIM GET A PROTECTIVE ORDER?

Victims can apply for a protective order through the district or county attorney, a private attorney or through a legal aid service program. The application must be filed in the county in which the victim or the offender lives. There are no minimum time limits to establish residency, and protective orders are available in every county in Texas. These potential resources may also assist victims.

WHAT IS CHILD ABUSE?

According to Chapter 261 of the Texas Family Code, child abuse is an act or omission (failure to act) that endangers or impairs a child's physical, mental or emotional health and development. Child abuse may take the form of physical or emotional injury, sexual abuse, sexual exploitation, physical neglect, medical neglect, or inadequate supervision.

The law specifically excludes "reasonable" discipline by the child's parent, guardian, or conservator. Corporal punishment is not in itself abusive under the law. An act or omission is abusive only if "observable and material impairment" occurs as a result, or if it causes "substantial harm," or exposes the child to risk of substantial harm.

Assessment of neglect, like physical and emotional abuse, hinges on whether it causes substantial harm or observable and material impairment. The law excludes from its definition of neglect any failure to provide for the child that is due to lack of financial resources. A child living in poverty is not a victim of neglect under the Texas Family Code, except in cases where relief has been offered and refused by the child's parent, guardian, or conservator.

Accidental injury or harm is also excluded from the definition of abuse. However, a person commits abuse if he or she places a child, or allows a child to be placed, in a situation where the child is exposed to "substantial risk" of injury or harm. The law also clearly states that a person commits abuse if he or she fails to make a reasonable effort to prevent another person from abusing a child. This provision applies to all forms of abuse, including physical and emotional abuse, sexual abuse, and neglect.

WHAT IS SEXUAL ABUSE?

Sexual abuse is defined in the Family Code as any sexual conduct harmful to a child's mental, emotional, or physical welfare, as well as failure to make a reasonable effort to prevent sexual conduct with a child. A person who compels or encourages a child to engage in sexual conduct commits abuse, and it is against the law to make or possess child pornography or to display such material to a child.

Child sexual abuse includes fondling, lewd or lascivious exposure or behavior, sodomy, oral copulation, penetration of a genital or anal opening by a foreign object, child pornography, child prostitution, and any other "sexual conduct harmful to a child's mental, emotional, or physical welfare." These acts may be forced upon the child or the child may be coaxed, seduced, or persuaded to cooperate. The absence of force or coercion does not diminish the abusive nature of the conduct, but, sadly, it may cause the child to feel responsible for what has occurred.

It may be worth noting that contentious divorces often spawn cross-allegations of sexual impropriety or sexual abuse. The focus may be on handling of bath-time or bed-time routines, or may center on a parent's dating behaviors or casual use of the internet. It may even lead to visits from Children's Protective Services at one or both households. If your interactions with your children are respectful and appropriate, such visits may actually be welcomed as a way of diffusing unwarranted allegations.

TYPES OF CHILD ABUSE

- *Physical Abuse*: "Physical injury that results in substantial harm to the child." The law excludes physical punishment that does not result in injury.

- *Emotional Abuse*: "Emotional injury to a child that results in an observable and material impairment in the child's growth, development, or psychological functioning."

- *Sexual Abuse*: "Sexual conduct harmful to a child's mental, emotional, or physical welfare."

- *Neglect*: "Leaving of a child in a situation where the child would be exposed to a substantial risk of physical or mental harm, without arranging for necessary care for the child." The law excludes failure to provide due to financial need, unless relief has been offered and refused.

REPORTING CHILD ABUSE

If you see, know of, or suspect abuse, call the state or local law enforcement authorities immediately. You must provide enough information to allow agents to locate the child. Your report may include names, address, license plate number, and make of car. If a child is in immediate danger of serious bodily harm, call 911 or local law enforcement immediately.

You are finished with the final lesson! Take the quiz to verify your understanding.

We congratulate you and wish you the best.

LESSON 13 QUIZ

1.   T / F   Victims of family violence need to have a witness before they can report the incident.

2.   T / F   The 911 hotline should be used to report rumors of family violence.

3.   T / F   Emotional abuse of a child is not currently covered by Texas law.

4.   T / F   Accidental injury to a child is not generally covered by law unless a child has been placed at risk.

5.   T / F   If you report an abusive situation, you must provide enough information to allow agents to locate the child.

6.   T / F   A child living in poverty is not legally a victim of abuse or neglect.

7.   T / F   When reporting abuse, it is better to use a national rather than a local hotline.

8.   T / F   An application for a protective order can be filed by a victim in any county of Texas, regardless of residence.

9.   T / F   A Texas resident filing a protective order must meet a minimum residency requirement.

10.   1T / F   A protective order for a child can restrict an offender from being near the victim's school.

RESOURCES

Ahrons, C. (1994) *The Good Divorce*. New York, NY: HarperCollins Publishers.

Benedek, E. (1995). *How to Help Your Child Overcome Your Divorce*. Arlington, VA: American Psychiatric Association.

Bienenfeld, F. (1996). *Helping Your Child Through Divorce*. Alameda, CA: Hunter House.

Blau, M. (1995) *Families Apart: Ten Keys to Successful Co-Parenting*. New York, NY: The Berkley Publishing Group.

Blau, M. (2010). *Consequential Strangers: Turning Everyday Encounters into Life-Changing Moments*. New York, NY: W. W. Norton & Company.

Bray, J. (1998) *Stepfamilies*. New York, NY: Broadway Books

Brazelton, T. (2006) *Touchpoints*. Cambridge, MA: Da Capo Press.

Cline, F. & Fay, J. (2006). *Parenting With Love & Logic*. Colorado Springs, CO: Piñon Press.

Ellis, E. (2000). *Divorce Wars: Interventions with Families in Conflict*. Washington, DC: American Psychological Association.

Emery, R. (2006). *The Truth about Children and Divorce: Dealing with the Emotions So You and Your Children Can Thrive*. New York, NY: Plume.

Everett, C. & Everett, S. (1994) *Healthy Divorce*. San Francisco, CA: Jossey-Bass Publishers.

Gold, L. (1995). *Between Love and Hate: A Guide to Civilized Divorce*. New York, NY: Plume.

Gottman, J. (1995). Why Marriages Succeed or Fail: And How You Can Make Yours Last. New York: Simon & Schuster.

Hatchett, G. (2003) *Say What You Mean and Mean What You Say!* New York, NY: HarperCollins Publishers.

Heegaard, M. (1996). *When Mom and Dad Separate: Children Can Learn to Cope with Grief from Divorce.* Bloomington, MN: Woodland Press.

Lansky, V. (2005) *Divorce Book for Parents.* Minnetonka, MN: Book Peddlars.

Lehman, J. (2004) *The Total Transformation Program.* Westbrook, ME: Legacy Publishing.

Nelson, J. (2006) *Positive Discipline.* New York, NY: Ballantine Books.

Neuman, M. (1999). *Helping Your Kids Cope with Divorce the Sandcastles Way.* New York: Random House.

Oddenino, M. (1996). *Putting Kids First: Walking Away From a Marriage without Walking Over the Kids.* Salt Lake City, UT: Family Connections Pub.

Pickhardt, C. (2005). *The Everything Parent's Guide to Children and Divorce.* Avon, MA: Adams Media.

Raser, Jaime. (1999) *Raising Children You Can Live With: A Guide for Frustrated Parents.* Houston, TX: Bayou Publishing.

Shulman, D. (1996). *Co-Parenting after Divorce: How to Raise Happy, Healthy Children in Two-Home Families.* Sherman Oaks, CA: Winnspeed Press.

Teyber, E. (2001). *Helping Children Cope with Divorce.* Hoboken, New Jersey: Jossey-Bass.

Wallerstein, J. and Kelly, J. (1996). *Surviving the Breakup: How Children and Parents Cope With Divorce.* New York, NY: Basic Books.

Wallerstein, J., Lewis, J., and Blakeslee, S. (2001) *The Unexpected Legacy of Divorce: The 25 Year Landmark Study.* New York, NY: Hachette Books.

INDEX

ABOUT THE AUTHOR

James A. (Jim) Baker is founder, former CEO, and current board chairman of Baker Communications, Inc., the Houston-based global leader in corporate training programs for over three decades, delivering focused, specialized training, strategy execution, and management development to over 50% of the Fortune 500. A celebrated corporate coach

and trainer, Jim is also a best-selling author, invited professor, senior business consultant, and speaker. Baker's company recently launched CloudCoaching International, a joint venture with acclaimed performance strategist Tony Robbins that utilizes interactive dynamic web-based training in sales and service performance management.

Jim received his B.S. from the University of Rochester, Behavioral Science Certification from the Rochester Institute of Technology, his M.S. from the State University of New York, and attended the South Texas College of Law. Jim is a co-founder of the National Center for Dispute Settlement of the American Arbitration Association, a past instructor for the Jesse H. Jones Graduate School of Business, Rice University, and an Adjunct Professor for the University of Houston

An active author and writer, Jim's books include The Anger Busting Training and Counseling Guide (Bayou Publishing), Selling Success: The Complete Sales 10.0 Game Plan and Positive Parenting (Bayou Publishing). He is a contributing author to The Sales Training Handbook: A Guide to Developing Sales Performance, published by Prentice Hall and sponsored by the American Society for Training and Development. He contributes monthly articles in the fields of Executive Presentation Skills, Negotiations Training, Time Management, Managing for Motivation, and Sales.

Baker resides with his wife, Xiao Rong Zhang, and their daughter, Nana, in the River Oaks area of Houston, Texas, and in Telluride, Colorado. He has two daughters by a previous marriage, Bridget Baker Rogers and Sarah Baker McConnell.

In addition to his professional accomplishments, Jim has been deeply involved in civic affairs for many years. He has distinguished himself as an active leader involved in numerous civic projects and serving on many corporate and non-profit boards and committees nationally, in Texas, and in the Greater Houston area, including:

- Advisory Board Member — Republican National Committee

- Board of Directors —Jewish Institute for National Security Affairs (JINSA)

- Board of Directors — Greater Houston Partnership

- Senior Consultant — DuPont Corporation

- Creator and Co-Founding Board Member — Houston Drug-Free Business Initiative

- Member, Board of Visitors — South Texas College of Law

- Member — Executive Committee of the Office for the Prevention of Developmental Disabilities (appointed by the Governor of Texas)

- Member — Statewide Media Task Force on Dropout Prevention (appointed by the Governor of Texas)

- Board of Directors — Harris County - Houston Sports Authority

- Board of Directors — Corporation for Economic Development of Harris County

- Board of Directors – Cenikor Foundation, Drug Rehabilitation Centers

- Founder & Chairman — The Anger Management Training Institute, LLC.

BOOKS BY JAMES A. (JIM) BAKER

The Anger Busting Workbook – Simple Powerful Techniques for Managing Anger and Saving Relationships
>   For more information on the online training programs, visit:
>   www.AngerManagementSeminar.com,
>   www.Anger-Management-Classes.net
>   www.BayouPublishing.com

The Counseling and Training Guide for the Anger Busting Workbook
>   For more information on this online training program for Anger Therapists, visit:
>   www.AngerManagementSeminar.com
>   www.BayouPublishing.com

The Sexual Harassment Workbook – Recognizing, Managing, and Preventing Sexual Harassment in the Workplace
>   For more information on the online training program, visit:
>   www.SexualHarassmentTraining.biz
>   www.BayouPublishing.com

Positive Parenting 101: A Handbook for Parents Undergoing Divorce
>   For more information on the online training program, visit:
>   www.Online-Class-Parenting-Divorce.com
>   www.BayouPublishing.com

The Ultimate Trainer's Handbook - Maximize Your Seminar Leadership Skills - Powerful tips, tools and strategies from a training expert
>   For more information on the online training program, visit:
>   www.Training-the-Trainer-Courses.com
>   www.BayouPublishing.com

Boating Safety Essentials Handbook
>   For more information on the online training program, visit:
>   www.Boating-Safety-Course.net
>   www.BayouPublishing.com

Zen and the Art of Negotiation - Becoming the Winning Negotiator You Already Are
>   www.BakerCommunications.com
>   www.BayouPublishing.com

The Tactical Negotiator – Simple, Effective Skills That Will Guarantee You the Edge in Any Negotiation
>   www.BakerCommunications.com
>   www.BayouPublishing.com

Sales 10.0 – Blocking and Tackling Your Way to the Top
>   www.BakerCommunications.com
>   www.BayouPublishing.com

Texas Cooking – Delicious Texas Recipes from the Grill to the Table
>   www.Texas-Cookin.com
>   www.BayouPublishing.com

ORDERING INFORMATION

Additional copies of **Positive Parenting 101** are available from the publisher. Orders may be placed by phone, by mail, by FAX, or directly on the web. Purchase orders from institutions are welcome.

- ❏ *To order by mail:* Complete this order form and mail it (along with check or credit card information) to Bayou Publishing, 2524 Nottingham, Houston, TX 77005-1412.

- ❏ *To order by phone:* Call (800) 340-2034.

- ❏ *To order by FAX:* Fill out this order form (including credit card information) and fax to (713) 526-4342.

- ❏ *To place a secure online order:* Visit http://www.bayoupublishing.com.

Name: _____

Address: _____

_____

City: _____ ST: __ Zip: _____

Ph: _____

FAX: _____

E-mail: _____

❏ VISA ❏ MasterCard ❏ American Express ❏ Discover

Charge Card #: _____

Expiration Date: _____

Signature: _____

Please send me ____ copies at $24.95 each _____

Sales Tax 8.25%(Texas residents) _____

plus $4.50 postage and handling *(per order)* _____ $4.50

Total $ _____

Bayou Publishing, LLC • 2524 Nottingham, Suite 150
Houston, TX 77005-1412
Ph: (713) 526-4558/ FAX: (713) 526-4342
Orders: (800) 340-203 4• http://www.bayoupublishing.com

Quantity discounts are available to your company or educational institution for reselling, educational purposes, subscription incentives, gifts or fundraising campaigns. For more information, please contact the publisher at 1-800-340-2034.